James VI and I

King of Great Britain

Irene Carrier

Withington Girls' School

CAMBRIDGE
UNIVERSITY PRESS

PUBLISHED BY THE PRESS SYNDICATE OF THE UNIVERSITY OF CAMBRIDGE
The Pitt Building, Trumpington Street, Cambridge CB2 1RP, United Kingdom

CAMBRIDGE UNIVERSITY PRESS
The Edinburgh Building, Cambridge CB2 2RU, United Kingdom
40 West 20th Street, New York, NY 10011-4211, USA
10 Stamford Road, Oakleigh, Melbourne 3166, Australia

First published 1998

Printed in the United Kingdom at the University Press, Cambridge

Typeset in Ehrhardt and Gill Sans

A catalogue record for this book is available from the British Library

ISBN 0 521 49947 X paperback

Layout and composition by Newton Harris

Acknowledgements

The author and publisher are grateful to the following for permission to reproduce photographs:
1.6a by permission of the British Library, T.14051(2); 1.18a by permission of the Trustees of
Dulwich Picture Gallery; 1.18b National Maritime Museum, London; 1.18c by courtesy of the
National Portrait Gallery, London, and the Marquess of Salisbury; 1.19 the Royal Collection © Her
Majesty the Queen; 1.20 by courtesy of the National Portrait Gallery, London; 1.21, 1.22, 1.23
Crown copyright: Historic Royal Palaces; 2.10 University of Glasgow (Glasgow University Media
Services Photographic Unit); 2.12a by permission of the British Library, Add Ms 48343; 2.12b ©
the British Museum.

The cover illustration is a portrait of James VI and I by Cornelius Janssen, from the Falkland Palace
collection (reproduced by kind permission of the National Trust for Scotland).

Every effort has been made to reach copyright holders. The publisher would be pleased to hear from
anyone whose rights they have unwittingly infringed.

To my family and friends,
to my teachers especially Joan Blyth
and the late Professor Rosalind Hill,
and my pupils

Contents

Acknowledgements

This book could never have been written without the help and support of a number of institutions and individuals. My greatest debt is to the British Library (North Library), where I spent every school holiday over the last few years and whose staff worked miracles for me, aware of the very real constraints imposed upon provincial readers. I am also much obliged to Michael Carrier for encouragement and the practical support of an academic librarian, without whom the index would have proved impossible, and to Douglas Webster for the meticulous proofreading that only a true scholar can provide. Comments made by John Morrill were gratefully received and acted upon, and the sixth form students of Withington Girls' School had a double input: I valued them as 'guinea pigs' for some of the more difficult material and was kept at the task by their genuine enthusiasm to see their teacher in print.

Irene Carrier
Salford, 1997

Introduction

James I King of Great Britain has in some ways been a victim of doubtful historical hypotheses. His very real achievements have been sacrificed to theories such as periodisation (the myth of the 'Age of Elizabeth') and linear progress (the Whig myth of the relentlessness of the progress of parliamentary power) and to the persuasiveness of hindsight ('high road to Civil War' theories).

The recent explosion in historical research (see Chapter 7) has made this monarch even more difficult for students to understand. Historians in the Whig tradition who saw Parliament 'gaining the initiative' over the Crown in his reign have been superseded by scholars whose research has revealed the great complexities in key areas such as Church, State and foreign affairs. Revisionists have stressed the non-confrontational nature of Jacobean Parliaments, effective compromise in religious issues and a degree of perspicacity in foreign affairs. Revisionism has inspired critical research which challenges both old and new ideas, enriching the historical debate.

This book is not designed as a James I compendium. For an introductory account of the reign with interpretation, S. J. Houston's book remains unchallenged – especially after its 1995 revision. This volume is produced in the firm belief that real understanding of a difficult period can be gained by studying primary source material in the context of wide reading and good teaching. These extracts are meant to inspire questions, research and, above all, discussion.

The material selected for each of the seven chapters represents issues of the period. The first chapter is devoted to making students really familiar with aspects of the character of James I; as the interpretation of his personality suffers from distortion, three perspectives are offered: that of his youth in Scotland, that of writers in the 1640s and 1650s and that of his immediate contemporaries.

The second chapter deals with James's greatest vision, that of the Union of England and Scotland. This is an area of research that is under great scrutiny at the moment (see Chapter 7); the relevance of the issue at a time of pressure for the disintegration of the United Kingdom and of the problems of European Union is obvious.

One of the vehicles through which James hoped to achieve union was that of religion (see Chapter 3). It is sometimes difficult for students today to appreciate the importance of religious conformity in the seventeenth century, and the degree of intolerance of that society is indeed abhorrent to many. We cannot and must not judge the age of James I by modern values, or the lack of them! He believed it essential to maintain unity in the state through religious conformity. This dimension was very important in the British perspective.

In his relations with Parliament (Chapter 4), James has come in for much criticism (see Chapter 7). Many of the issues raised in the parliamentary arena are dealt with in detail in other chapters (e.g. finance in Chapter 5 and foreign policy in Chapter 6). This means that the extracts on Crown–Parliament relations focus rather on issues of prerogative and privilege. This seems justified in view of the fact that, during James's whole reign as King of Great Britain, Parliament was in session for only thirty-six months.

In many ways the year 1618 was to prove a catalyst for James. The constant weakness of his rule had proved to be that of finance (Chapter 5). The outbreak that year of the Thirty Years War involving his own dynastic policies brought to a head the problems that had earlier plagued him: those of money, religion, foreign policy and prerogative. By 1624 money for foreign policy could come only from Parliament, and King James knew as well as anybody the potential consequences of this. There is no argument for saying that by 1624 James was old, ill and no longer cared about the direction of foreign policy. James remained politically astute to the end of his life.

Each of the seven chapters has a short introduction and linking material. Each is preceded by a time chart and ends with a recommended reading list, where appropriate. The most rewarding procedure is for students to read round each topic, then study the extracts and discuss the questions.

1 'The wisest fool in Christendom'

Time chart	
Significant events in the formation of the character of King James VI and I	

1566	*19 June:* born
1567	Murder of his father, Lord Darnley
	Abdication of his mother, Mary Queen of Scots
	29 July: became James VI of Scotland; Earl of Moray Regent
1568	Flight of Mary to England
1570	Assassination of Moray
	Earl of Lennox Regent
1571	Lennox killed
	Earl of Mar Regent
1572	Earl of Morton became Regent after death of Mar
1579	Visit of Esmé Stuart
1580	Fall of the Earl of Morton
1584	Earl of Arran in power
1584	*Essays of a Prentise on the Divine Art of Poesy*
1585	Fall of Arran
1586	League with England
1587	Execution of Mary Queen of Scots
1589	Marriage to Anne of Denmark
1594	Birth of Prince Henry
1596	Birth of Princess Elizabeth
1597	*Demonologie*
1598	*Trew Law*
1599	*Basilikon Doron*
1600	Birth of Prince Charles
1603	Accession to the English throne as James I

1604	*Counterblaste to Tobacco*
1607	*Apologie for the Oath of Allegiance* Robert Carr favourite
1612	Death of Cecil and of Prince Henry
1613	Marriage of Elizabeth to Frederick of the Rhine Palatinate
1614	George Villiers favourite
1616	*Collected Works*
1619	Death of Queen Anne *A Remonstrance of King James for the Rights of Kings and Independence of their Crowns*
1625	Death of King James

The over-quoted witticism of the chapter title, dubiously attributed to Henry IV of France, is accurate only in one respect: it indicates the sharp contrasts to be found in the very complex character of this monarch. G. P. V. Akrigg, in his edition of *The Letters of King James VI and I*, wrote: 'It is not enough to salute King James as an original – he was also one of the most complicated neurotics ever to sit on either the English or the Scottish throne.'

He was certainly the most learned ruler of the three kingdoms; his literary output was diverse and considerable, encompassing religion, political theory and witchcraft (see the time chart at the beginning of this chapter). His hatred of violence and persecution makes him sympathetic to the modern reader, who is also more charitable towards his lack of physical beauty and his preference for young men. His turbulent childhood was hardly designed to produce emotional stability. While in the womb he experienced trauma as his mother was forced to watch the murder of her secretary, David Rizzio; within a year of his birth his father, Lord Darnley, had been murdered and his mother, Mary Queen of Scots, was forced to abdicate and throw herself upon the mercy of Elizabeth of England, leaving the thirteen-month-old James as King of Scotland in 1567. A succession of regents despatched by either assassins or intrigue engendered a real rather than paranoid fear of violence in the young king. The rigorous education provided by George Buchanan stretched his mind; the visit of his French kinsman, Esmé Stuart, developed the emotions of the fourteen-year-old king, possibly awakening homosexual feelings and emotional dependence noticed long before the arrival of George Villiers. Elizabeth I of England's execution of his mother in 1587, and determination to make him wait for the southern kingdom, tested his patience and diplomacy to the full.

The starting point for analysis [1.1] is the pen sketch of James sent to the French secretary of Mary Queen of Scots by M. de Fontenay, who visited Edinburgh in 1584. It is a distillation of what information the author felt appropriate for the exiled queen. It was written almost twenty years before James acquired the southern kingdom.

De Fontenay raised the question of James's attitude to his mother. Her execution strengthened his rule in Scotland and demonstrated his diplomacy [1.2, 1.3]. It also confirmed his belief that his destiny was to revive the ancient empire of Britannia as a new Brutus [2.1].

Almost twenty-five years after James's death and nearly seventy-five years after the assessment of de Fontenay, the ripest source for the character of James appeared. This was the creation of the pseudo-wit Sir Anthony Weldon, a man demonstrably too clever by half, a man whose scurrilous scribblings on Scotland in 1617 [2.22] had cost him his court post, and whose *Court and Character of King James* may be seen as a character assassination. However, Weldon had died in 1648 and, according to Sanderson in his *Complete History* published in 1656, was not personally responsible for the publication of his manuscript, 'which with some regret of what he had maliciously writ, intended to the fire, and died repentant, though since stolen to the press out of a ladies closet'.

James's satirists and caricaturists found a receptive audience for their printed word during the early years of the Interregnum – the English Republic, which lasted from 1649 to 1660. Weldon's manuscript [1.4] appeared publicly in 1650, *A Cat May Look upon a King* [1.6] in 1652, and Wilson's *Life and Reign of James, The First King of Great Britain* [1.7] in 1653. Weldon and Wilson show how the features identified by de Fontenay in 1584 have by the 1650s become distorted by cruel caricature, pretentious style and slavish political correctness. Regrettably, such scribblings have provided the popular image of James I of Great Britain. Although Sanderson and Aulicus Coquinariae [1.5] – probably the same author – wrote specifically to discredit the character painted by Weldon, they lack wit and so have not proved memorable.

A reasonable balance is achieved in the appraisal by the royalist, Sir John Oglander [1.8]. While he depicts James's all too familiar traits – aversion to violence, vulnerability in front of strangers or crowds, and preference for young men – these characteristics are set against his judgement and scholarship. In Oglander, more than in any other source, the earthy wit of the king, the coarse vulgar streak, is seen clearly but in a way that makes James more human and less of a caricature.

There are common characteristics to be seen in writers looking from such different perspectives as his early years in Scotland and the Interregnum [1.1–1.8]. Observers who wrote during his reign as King of Great Britain, and his own letters during that period, support the notion of the complexity of his character. They show him timorous, impulsive, socially ill at ease, financially inept, emotionally immature and with a predisposition towards male favourites [1.14–1.17]. They show him as intelligent, perceptive, a patron of arts and an astute wit. What is at issue is not mere characteristics, but questions of degree and extent, both in contemporary sources and sources in more distant perspectives. His uncertain temperament is best understood through a study of his health provided by his physician [1.13].

It is significant that many of the character studies describe James's physical appearance. Nowadays we divorce character from physical appearance; in the early seventeenth century the form and feature of the body were believed to reflect the mind and soul, making physical defects quick to be seized upon by hostile writers. Such verbal portraits tell us more about the authors than the subject, albeit they remain the essential source material.

The study of the character of the king will be extended throughout the book. This chapter ends with a short introduction to the ways in which his character has been portrayed and revealed in the visual arts and architecture [1.18–1.23].

The investigation into the character of James has drawn upon many sources. Testimony has rarely been impartial; frequently it has been refracted by the prevailing political correctness of the 1630s, late 1640s and 1650s. James I may, in the words of the author of *1066 and All That*, have 'slobbered at the mouth and had favourites', but he was neither a fool nor a 'bad king'.

1.1 M. de Fontenay reports on James as King of Scotland to the French secretary of Mary Queen of Scots, Edinburgh, 15 August 1584

My brother, the letter which follows will remain secret between you and me.

The King received me very well; he treated me better in effect than in appearance; he gave me much credit without many caresses … At one thing only I am astonished, he has never inquired anything of the Queen [Mary Queen of Scots] or of her health, or her treatment, her servants, her living and eating, her recreation, or anything similar,   5
and nevertheless I know that he loves and honours her very much in his heart. To tell you freely what I have known of him … He has three parts of the soul in perfection. He grasps and understands quickly; he judges carefully and with reasonable discourses; he restrains himself well and for long. In his demands he is quick and piercing, and determined in his replies. Of what ever things they dispute, whether it   10
be religion or anything else, he believes and maintains always what seems to him most true and just … He is learned in many languages, sciences, and affairs of state – I dare say more than all those of his kingdom. In short he has a marvellous spirit –

for the rest full of virtuous glory and good opinion of himself. Having been
nourished in fear he has still this fault, that he often dare not contradict the great   15
lords, and nevertheless he likes very much to be considered brave and to be feared …
He hates dancing and music in general … His ways for want of being well instructed
are very rude and uncivil in speaking, eating … and entertainment in the company of
women. He never stops in one place, taking a singular pleasure in walking, but his
gait is bad, composed of erratic steps, and he tramps about even in his room. He has   20
a loud voice, and is very grave in his words. He likes hunting above all the pleasures
of the world, remaining there at least six hours together chasing all over the place
with loosened rein … I have only noticed in him three things very bad for the
preservation of his state and the government of the same. The first is his ignorance
and lack of knowledge of his poverty and his little strength, promising too much of   25
himself and despising other princes. The second, that he loves indiscreetly and
inadvisedly in spite of his subjects. The third is that he is too lazy and too thoughtless
over his affairs, too willing and devoted to his pleasure, especially hunting, leaving his
affairs to be managed by the Earl of Arran, Montrose and his Secretary. I know well
that this is excusable at his young age, but it is to be feared that continuance will   30
confirm him in this habit.

… [However] he told me that no affair of importance ever happened of which he did
not know, although he did not seem to. And although he spent much of his time in
hunting he could do as much business in one hour as others could in a day, because
simultaneously he listened and spoke, watched, and sometimes did five things at   35
once. That nothing was done secretly by the lords that he did not know, by means of
having spies at the doors of their rooms morning and evening, who came and
reported everything to him. For the rest, he is the true son of his mother in many
things, but principally in that he is weak in body and cannot work long at his affairs,
but when he gives himself to it he does more than six others together, adding that   40
sometimes he has wished to force and keep himself six days continually at accounts,
but that immediately after he never fails to be ill.

Calendar of State Papers relating to Scotland and Mary Queen of Scots,
1547–1603, ed. W. K. Boyd, vol. 7, 1913, pp. 273–75

Questions

1   How reliable is this letter as a source of information on the character of
    James? As you make your judgement, consider the author of the report,
    the purpose of it, for whom it was intended, and its date.
2   Do the positive aspects of the king's character outweigh the negative
    aspects?
3   Which of the negative aspects do you consider to be most serious in a
    king of Scotland in the late sixteenth century?
4   Why, in your opinion, does the writer dwell on the king's physical
    appearance?

James's attitude to the execution of his mother

1.2 Instructions by James VI to the Master of Gray, 17 December 1586

You shall in our name signify to our dearest sister the Queen of England that we marvel not a little of the late preposterous and strange procedure against the Queen our dearest mother, who being a sovereign princess, and in all degrees of the best blood in Europe, has been by subjects judged both in life and title, a dangerous precedent for all princes, and without any approved example in any age or Kingdom,   5 and so contrary to our honour as hardly could anything have fallen out so prejudicial thereunto …

You shall explain to our said dearest sister with what just grief we have heard of the rigour intended against our dearest mother, and that nothing in this world is more dear unto us than her life …

R. S. Rait and A. I. Cameron, *King James's Secret*, 1927, pp. 107, 114

1.3 Letter from James VI to Elizabeth I, 26 January 1587

What thing, madame, can greatlier touch me in honour that [am] a king and a son that my nearest neighbour, being in straitest [friend]ship with me, shall rigorously put to death a free sovereign prince and my natural mother, alike in estate and sex to her that so uses her, albeit subject I grant to harder fortune, and touching her nearly in proximity of blood. What law of God can permit that justice shall strike upon   5 them whom he has appointed supreme dispensators of the same under him, whom he hath called gods and therefore subjected to the censure of none on earth, whose anointing by God cannot be defiled by man unrevenged by the author thereof, who, being supreme and immediate lieutenants of God in heaven, cannot therefore be judged by their equals on earth? What monstrous thing is it that sovereign princes   10 themselves should be the example-givers of their own sacred diadems profaning?

The Letters of King James VI and I, ed. G. P. V. Akrigg, 1984, no. 26

Questions

1 What information do the letters [1.2, 1.3] give about James's attitude to his mother?
2 How far do the letters support the view of M. de Fontenay on this matter?
3 What do the letters reveal of James VI's ideas about the nature of monarchy?

James I from the historical perspective of the English republic

1.4 The king's appearance and character

This King's character is much easier to take than his picture, for he could never be brought to sit for the taking of that, which is the reason of so few good pieces of him; but his character was obvious to every eye.

He was of a middle stature, more corpulent through his clothes than in his body, yet fat enough, his clothes ever being made large and easy, the doublets quilted for   5 stiletto proof, his breeches in pleats and full stuffed. He was naturally of a timorous disposition, which was the reason of his quilted doublets; his eye large, ever rolling after any stranger came into his presence, in so much as many for shame have left the room, as being out of countenance; his beard was very thin; his tongue too large for his mouth, which ever made him speak full in the mouth, and made him drink very   10 uncomely, as if eating his drink ... his skin was as soft as taffeta sarsnet, which felt so, because he never washed his hands, only rubbed his finger ends slightly with the wet end of a napkin, his legs were very weak, having as was thought some foul play in his youth, or rather before he was born, that he was not able to stand at seven years of age, that weakness made him ever leaning on other men's shoulders; his walk was   15 ever circular, his fingers ever in that walk, fiddling about his codpiece ... He was very constant in all things (his favourites excepted) in which he loved change, yet never cast down any (he once raised) from the height of greatness ... unless by their own default ... He was ever best when furthest from the Queen ... He naturally loved not the sight of a soldier, nor of any valiant man ...   20

He was very witty, and had as many ready witty jests as any man living, at which he would not smile himself, but deliver them in a grave and serious manner: He was very liberal, of what he had not in his own gripe, and would rather part with £100 he never had in his keeping; than one twenty shillings piece within his own custody ...

He was so crafty and cunning in petty things ... as a very wise man was wont to say   25 he believed him the wisest fool in Christendom, meaning him wise in small things, but a fool in weighty affairs ...

He was infinitely inclined to peace, but more out of fear than conscience, and this (fear) was the greatest blemish this king had through all his reign, otherwise might have been ranked with the very best of our kings.   30

In a word, take him altogether and not in pieces, such a King I wish this kingdom have never any worse, on the condition, not any better; for he lived in peace, died in peace, and left all his kingdoms in a peaceable condition, with his own motto: Beati Pacifici.[1]

[1] Beati Pacifici = 'Blessed are the Peacemakers'

Sir Anthony Weldon, *The Court and Character of King James*, **1650, pp. 177ff.**

1.5 A defence of the king

Was ever Prince thus limn'd[1] out to posterity, by his quilted doublets, and full stuffed breeches? Who reads his Court needs none of this Character; so like they are in belying. But I spare the author, and pity the Publisher – the deficiency of the one, could not make out the other. For it becomes the wit of man, in truth, to apprehend King James, whose wisdom in his sovereignty, had esteem beyond any contemporary Potentate, with his reign.   5

[1] limn'd = painted or sketched

Attributed to Sanderson, *Aulicus Coquinariae: or a Vindication in Answer to a Pamphlet entitled the Court and Character of King James*, **1650, pp. 200–01**

Questions

1   With what justification might Weldon's work **[1.4]** be seen as a character assassination of James I?
2   Examine the similarities and differences of the accounts presented by de Fontenay **[1.1]** and that of Weldon.
3   How convincing do you find the Vindication offered by Sanderson as a refutation of Weldon's *Court and Character*?

1.6 A satirical tract

1.6(a)

The title page of the tract A Cat May Look upon a King *shows a cat looking at a portrait of James I in an oval circumscribed by his motto 'Beati Pacifici'. Underneath, the inscription reads 'Mars, Puer, Alecto, Virgo,* VULPES*, Leo, Nullus'. An identical engraving of James and inscriptions are to be found on the title page of the 1650*

edition of Weldon's Court and Character. *The second inscription refers to a prophecy of succession of Kings and Queens in England from Henry VIII (Mars) until the Commonwealth (Nullus). James I is called* VULPES *(fox) to indicate his craftiness. (Weldon had emphasised that James held dissimulation to be the 'craft' of kings.)*

1.6(b)

And surely I find (by the help of my spectacles) King James was the fountain of all our late afflictions and miseries ...

For his person, a man might sufficiently and truly make a volume, only to tell of his laziness, and his uncleanness; but I cannot do it without fouling too much paper.

He was a great pretender to learning and religion, and for the speculative part, had   5
as much as any of our Kings upon record; but for the practical, and the best part of it (if we may judge the tree by his fruit) we may without breach of charity conclude him not guilty. He was the greatest blasphemer in the world; swear faster than speak, and curse the people by the clock ...

The King was naturally fearful ... And what he would do, and durst not own, that he   10
would do by his Favourites, whom (for the fitness of his designs) he would raise from low degree, to oblige them the more, and to desert them the more, and shift them often till he had them fitted to his purpose ...

This King had no wars; but spent more money prodigally, profusely and riotously than any of his predecessors. What swarms of Scots came with him, and after him,   15
into this kingdom? Who perpetually sucked him of most vast sums of monies ... which put him upon all dishonourable ways of raising monies, to the most cruel oppression of this nation, to serve their riot and luxury.

Both 1.6(a) and (b) from *A Cat May Look upon a King*, **1652 (British Library Tract)**

1.7 Royal visits: uneasy public relations

The King's first going abroad (1603) was privately to visit some of his houses, for naturally he did not love to be looked on; and those formalities of state, which set a lustre upon Princes in the people's eyes, were but so many burdens to him; for his private recreations at home, and his hunting exercises abroad, both with the least disturbance, were his delight. While he remained in the Tower, he took pleasure in   5
baiting lions; but when he came abroad, he was so troubled with swarms [crowds], that he feared to be baited by people ... He was not like his predecessor, the late Queen, of famous memory, that with a well-pleased affection met her people's acclamations ...

Arthur Wilson, *The Life and Reign of James, the First King of Great Britain,* **1653, in** *A Complete History of England with the Lives of all the Kings and Queens thereof from the Earliest Account of Time to the Death of his Late Majesty William III,* **vol. 2, p. 667**

Questions

1 What are the common themes in the satires of James I in extracts **1.4**, **1.6** and **1.7**?
2 Compare the defects in his appearance and character noted by M. de Fontenay with those highlighted by **1.4**, **1.6** and **1.7**. Discuss the proposition that the defects are real and that the difference lies largely in the manner of treatment by the authors.
3 Why were the 1650s prolific years for satirising James I? Can you suggest reasons why James I rather than Charles I received such treatment?

1.8 A royalist's view

King James the first of England was the most cowardly man that ever I knew. He could not endure a soldier or to see men drilled, to hear of war was death to him, and how he tormented himself with fear of some sudden mischief may be proved by his great quilted doublets, pistol proof, as also his strange eyeing of strangers with a continual fearful observation ... Otherwise he was absolutely the best scholar and   5
wisest prince for general knowledge that ever England had, very merciful and passionate, liberal and honest. He was wondrous just between parties and had a very tender conscience ... He was the chastest prince for women that ever was, for he would often swear that he had never known any other woman than his wife ... For the present delivery of his mind he was the best of that age ... He had many witty   10
jests and also, in his passion, many profane. A great politician, and very sound in the reformed religion ... His facile good nature, being abused through the flattery of his courtiers, drew him to a greater rein of liberality than by nature he was inclined ... He was excessively taken with hunting, although in his latter time, by reason he could not ride fast, he had little pleasure in the chase ... His only faults were that he   15
was infinitely impatient, in which humour he would not forbear profanity. Secondly, he loved young men, his favourites, better than women, loving them beyond the love of men to women ... He was not popular nor plausible to his subjects that desired to see him. He could not endure to be seen of the commons, especially at his sports. If they came to see him in troops, as they usually did to Queen Elizabeth ... he would   20
cry out in Scottish, 'God's wounds! I will pull down my breeches and they shall see my arse!'

Sir John Oglander, *A Royalist's Notebook*, **ed. Francis Bamford, 1936, p. 193**

James I in the immediate perspective

1.9 Report on England presented by Nicolo Molin, Venetian ambassador, to the Government of Venice in 1607

He is sufficiently tall, of a noble presence, his physical constitution robust, and he is at pains to preserve it by taking much exercise at the chase, which he passionately loves, and uses not only as a recreation, but as a medicine. For this he throws off all business, which he leaves to his Council and to his Ministers. And so one may truly say that he is Sovereign in name and in appearance rather than in substance and   5
effect. This is the result of his deliberate choice, for he is capable of governing, being a Prince of intelligence and culture above the common, thanks to his application to and pleasure in study when he was young, though he has now abandoned that pursuit altogether.

Calendar of State Papers Venetian, vol. 10, 1900, p. 510

1.10 Part of a letter from James I to Robert Cecil, Viscount Cranborne, at the time of the Anglo-Scottish union negotiations, 22 November 1604

I could have heartily wished the day if it had been possible that my little beagle[1] had been stolen here in the likeness of a mouse, as he is not much bigger, to have been partaker of the sport which I had this day at hawking. There should ye have seen ... so well-flying Scottish hawks upon English fowls as ye could not have discerned but that they had been already naturalised without any reservation.

[1] my little beagle = James's nickname for Robert Cecil

Akrigg, *Letters*, no. 110

1.11 Part of a letter from James I to the Privy Council, 9 January 1605

We thought good ... to give some such directions for the execution of your places in our absence[1] as may supply any lack or inconvenience likely to arise in the managing of our affairs during the short times which we shall think fit to spend abroad from those places which are most commodious for the ordinary residence of our Council and officers of estate, from whom (as our subordinate ministers) so many men are to   5
receive rules and directions, as well concerning our own public and private services as for the universal satisfaction of our subjects, every man according to his particular occasions.

[1] James was about to leave for hunting after the Whitehall Christmas festivities.

Akrigg, *Letters*, no. 114

1.12 Part of a letter from James I to Robert Cecil, Viscount Cranborne, February 1605

And assure them (the Privy Council) that I shall never take longer vacancy from them for the necessary maintenance of my health than other kings will consume upon their physical diets and going to their whores.

Akrigg, *Letters*, no. 118

Questions

1   What evidence is there in extracts **1.10**, **1.11** and **1.12** that James I does not neglect the business of state when engaged in hunting?
2   How reliable is that evidence?
3   James insisted that hunting was a 'medicine' to him **[1.9, line 3]**. How acceptable do you find that explanation?

His mood was much affected by his health. His personal physician, Dr Theodore Mayerne, wrote a very detailed memoir on the health of James in 1623, a crucial year in his reign – especially in foreign affairs. Mayerne shows the king's great susceptibility to stress and provides evidence to indicate that some of his outbursts had physical origins.

1.13 Dr Theodore Mayerne's memoir on the king's health, drawn up December 1623

He is easily affected by cold and suffers in cold and damp weather ... The stomach is always ready for the burden of a large quantity ... Skin thin and delicate, so that it itches easily ... All functions naturally good, but perverted on occasion and most from disturbance of mind ... As regards food he does not much amiss except this that he eats no bread. He generally takes roast meats. Owing to want of teeth he does   5
not chew his food but bolts it. Fruit he eats at all hours of day and night. In drink he errs as to quality, quantity, frequency, time and order ... He has the strongest antipathy to water and all watery drinks. The King used to be given up to most violent exercise in hunting. Now he is quieter and lies or sits more, but that is due to the weakness of his knee-joints ... His mind is easily moved suddenly. He is very   10
wrathful, but the fit soon passes off ... Urine generally normal and sufficient. Often sandy sediment after a time ... He sweats easily owing to the thinness of his skin ... From the year 1619, after a severe illness, in which leeches were applied, (he) has had a copious haemorrhoidal flow almost daily. If this does not occur, the King becomes very irascible, melancholy, jaundiced, glows with heat and his appetite falls off. When   15
the flow returns all things are changed for the better ... In 1612 ... after the death of his son, a paroxysm[1] of melancholy – an attack of illness ending in diarrhoea lasting a few days. In 1619, after the Queen's death, pain in joints and nephritis with thick

sand … Fainting, sighing, dread, incredible sadness, intermittent pulse … Nephritis,
from which without any remedy having been administered, he excreted a friable   20
calculus[2]. The force of this, the most dangerous illness which the King ever had,
lasted for eight days … Many years ago, after hunting and long riding he often had
turbid urine and red like Alicant wine (which are His Majesty's words), but without
pain. July 12, 1613, bloody urine, with red sand … frequent vomiting and other
nephritic symptoms. The same, but worse, August … In 1615, October, the same   25
symptoms … Arthritis – Pains many years since invaded first the right foot, which
had an odd twist when walking … He demands relief and freedom from pain, little
considering about the causes of his illness. As to remedies:– The King laughs at
medicine, and holds it so cheap that he declares physicians to be of very little use and
hardly necessary. He asserts the art of medicine to be supported by mere conjectures,   30
and useless because uncertain.

[1] paroxysm = fit
[2] friable calculus = a stone that had broken up

**Norman Moore, *History of the Study of Medicine in the British Isles*, 1908,
pp. 97–106**

Questions

1   How far could Mayerne's memoir be used to explain some of the less
    attractive characteristics of James depicted in Weldon [1.4]?
2   Modern medical opinion suggests that James suffered from porphyria, a
    disturbance of the metabolic system which causes severe pain, red urine
    and great stress upon the nervous system. In what ways does Mayerne
    indicate a deterioration in the king's health in the later years of the reign?
3   In the light of your knowledge of the period, why would this
    deterioration in health be particularly important after 1618?

The Buckingham era

As James aged, his attraction towards youth and hatred of hassle increased.
George Villiers, later Duke of Buckingham, first caught the king's eye in 1614
when the king was growing weary of the current favourite, Somerset [1.15],
and the Protestant faction at court was keen to promote a favourite they could
control. While recent research asserts that the influence of Villiers on policy
was more apparent than real, his presence did little for the king's image [1.15,
1.16]. The many long letters from Francis Bacon to Villiers, including the
famous 'Advice', indicate that Villiers was something more than a political
lightweight. Bacon's instinct for climbing and his wish for political survival in
1621 [5.27] made him turn to Villiers for help.

1.14 Bacon's advice to Villiers, 1616

You are not only a courtier, but a bed-chamber man, and so are in the eye and ear of your master; but you are also a Favourite, the favourite of the time, and so are in his bosom also …

You are as a new-risen star, and the eyes of all men are upon you: let not your own negligence make you fall like a meteor.

[Bacon then offered advice at considerable length on how Villiers should organise his petitions in the following eight orders]

1 Matters concerning Religion …   2 Matters concerning Justice, the Laws …
3 Councillors, the Council Table, and great offices and officers of the kingdom.
4 Foreign negotiations and embassies.   5 Peace and War …   6 Trade, both at home and abroad.   7 Colonies and foreign plantations.   8 The Court …

The Letters and Life of Francis Bacon, ed. J. Spedding, vol. 6, 1872, pp. 30–31

1.15 Edward Hyde[1] on the ascendancy of Villiers

King James … began to be weary of his favourite, the earl of Somerset … who had been privy to a horrible murder … Mr Villiers appeared in court and drew the king's eyes upon him. There were enough in court angry against Somerset, for being what they themselves desired to be, and especially for being a Scotsman, to contribute all they could to promote one, that they might throw out the other …   5

Villiers was knighted, made a gentleman of the bedchamber, knight of the garter; and in a short time he was made baron, a viscount, an earl, a marquis, lord high admiral of England, master of the horse, and entirely disposed of all the graces of the king, in conferring all the honours and all the offices of the three kingdoms … he so exalted almost all of his numerous family and dependants, who had no other virtue or merit   10 than their alliance to him, which equally offended the ancient nobility, and the people of all conditions, who saw the flowers of the crown everyday fading and withered; whilst the … revenue thereof was sacrificed to enriching a private family.

[1] Hyde, later Earl of Clarendon, was a contemporary of George Villiers, Duke of Buckingham; his *History* was, however, written after the Restoration.

Edward Hyde, Earl of Clarendon, *Selections from the History of the Great Rebellion,* **ed. G. Huehns, 1978, p. 92**

1.16 Sir Anthony Weldon on Buckingham

And now Buckingham … swells in the height of pride; summons up all his country kindred, [his mother] providing a place for them to learn to carry themselves in a court-like garb; but, because they could not learn the French dances, country dances (for their sake only) must be the garb of the court, and none else must be used.

Then must these women-kindred be married to earls, earls' eldest sons, barons, or   5 chief gentlemen of great estates, insomuch, that the very female kindred were so numerous, as were sufficient to have peopled any plantation.

Weldon, *Court and Character,* **1650**

1.17 Letter to George Villiers, Marquis of Buckingham, *c.* 1622

My only sweet and dear child,

I am now so miserable a coward, as I do nothing but weep and mourn; for I protest to God, I rode this afternoon a great way in the park without speaking to anybody, and the tears trickling down my cheeks, as now they do, that I can scarcely see to write. But, alas! what shall I do at our parting? The only small comfort that I can have will   5 be to pry into thy defects with the eye of an enemy, and of every mote to make a mountain; and so harden my heart against thy absence. But this little malice is like jealousy, proceeding from a sweet root; but in one point it overcometh it, for, as it proceeds from love, so it cannot but end in love ...

James R

Intimate Letters of England's Kings, **ed. M. Sanders, 1959, p. 61**

Questions

1   Using the information in **1.14–1.17**, assess the significance of the influence of Villiers in domestic affairs during the reign of James I.
2   In the light of the above extracts and your own knowledge, discuss the view that Buckingham's influence was more apparent than real.

The iconography of James I, King of Great Britain

To test whether appearance illuminates character, a range of portraits of James may be examined. There are three major limitations to the value of this: first, James inherited the Elizabethan artistic isolation from mainstream Catholic continental art; second, he lacked the services of Rubens and Van Dyck that were available to his son. (Janssen, de Critz, Gheeraerts, Blijenberch and Van Somer generated some rather wooden portraits of James VI and I. Mytens made the king look much more human; all lacked the flair and style of Rubens and Van Dyck.) The third limitation is based on a character trait: James was impatient and hated posing for portraits. This is supported by Weldon [1.4], who spoke of a positive aversion to sitting; this is also mentioned by a number of other sources.

The de Critz genre of portraits [1.18] support the idea that James was very awkward, possibly feeling exposed, when sitting for a portrait. He wears the jewel known as The Mirror of Great Britain and this, together with the Garter insignia, indicates portraits made after the Union of Scotland and England. De Critz was active as court painter during the early years of James's reign as King of Great Britain. The portrait by Van Somer [1.19] is more revealing. A number of attributes indicate kingship; certainly James wished to stress the authority of his office. In the background, however, the artist is making the statement that this particular king was the patron of one of the greatest architectural constructions of the century, the Banqueting House at Whitehall [1.23]. So proud was James of this that it was shown in this portrait dating from about 1620, which was before the completion of the Banqueting House in 1622. The most famous state portrait is probably that by Daniel Mytens in 1621 [1.20]. It shows the king seated full length in the Garter robes. The rich crimson colour is contrasted with the white satin. Above James is the Tudor rose, confirming the legitimacy of his succession, and his motto 'Beati Pacifici'. He manages to look not only ill at ease, but also ill. Mayerne's report on his health [1.13] was roughly contemporary with this portrait.

Four years after his death, his son commissioned the Banqueting House ceiling from Rubens. The rich, flowing lines of these panels are full of allegory and symbolism. The clumsiness indicated in early written sources and wooden Jacobean portraiture has vanished. Rubens was doing for James I after his death what Van Dyck did for Charles I during his lifetime. James appears benevolent, wise, the architect of the Union of Britain [1.21], the bringer of peace and plenty (rather than a timorous financial idiot) who eventually took his place among the gods [1.22]. Without the constraints of a reluctant sitter, Rubens elevated James with elements of the Renaissance and the Baroque. While it reflects the aspirations of James, it is of the genre of temple decoration rather than portraiture; it shows the British Solomon rather than the 'wisest fool in Christendom'. It was commissioned during Charles I's peace negotiations with Spain in 1629 and was in place in the Banqueting House by 1635, the height of the Personal Rule of Charles. While this iconography was, in its own way, as biased as the anti-James writings of the Interregnum, it should not be forgotten that the building that housed these glorious images of the monarchy of James was his achievement as patron of its architect, Inigo Jones, and that the masques by Ben Jonson and others that were performed there were written as a direct result of his patronage.

1.18(a) John de Critz, *James I*, c. 1606

1.18(b) John de Critz, *James I*, after 1604

1.18(c) Attributed to John de Critz after Paul Van Somer, *James I*, 1623

1.19 Paul Van Somer, *James I*, *c.* 1620

1.20 Daniel Mytens, *James I and VI*, 1621

1.21 Sir Peter Paul Rubens, *The Union of England and Scotland under James I*, commissioned 1629 (The Banqueting House, Whitehall)

1.22 Sir Peter Paul Rubens, *The Apotheosis of James I*, commissioned 1629 (The Banqueting House, Whitehall)

1.23 The Banqueting House at Whitehall, completed 1622

Questions

1 What impressions of James I are conveyed by **1.18**, **1.19** and **1.20**? By what means are those messages conveyed?

2 How much do these portraits contribute to your knowledge of the king's character? Bear in mind that when you study a painting you should be aware of the purposes of the portrait, the stylistic conventions of the painter, and the audience for which the painting was designed.

Recommended reading

R. Ashton, *James I by his Contemporaries*, 1969

S. J. Houston, *James I*, 2nd edn, 1995

M. Lee Jr, *Great Britain's Solomon: James VI and I in his Three Kingdoms*, 1990

M. Lee Jr, 'James I and the historians: not a bad king after all?', *Albion*, vol. 16, 1984

R. Lockyer, *Buckingham: The Life and Political Career of George Villiers, First Duke of Buckingham*, 1981

D. Mathew, *James I*, 1967

A. G. R. Smith, *The Reign of James VI and I*, 1973

D. H. Willson, *King James VI and I*, 1956

K. Hearn (ed.), *Dynasties: Painting in Tudor and Jacobean England, 1530–1630*, 1995

S. Morris, *A Teacher's Guide to Using Portraits*, 1989

R. Strong, *Britannia Triumphans: Inigo Jones, Rubens and Whitehall Palace*, 1980

R. Strong, *The English Icon: Elizabethan and Jacobean Portraiture*, 1969

2 'I am the husband; the whole isle is my lawful wife.' The union of two kingdoms

Time chart	
1578	The claim of the Countess of Lennox (James's grandmother) to the English throne passed to James
1587	Execution of Mary Queen of Scots
1600	Exchanges of letters between Robert Cecil and James VI began to prepare the way for James's smooth accession to the English throne
1603	Death of Elizabeth of England and the accession of James to the English throne as James I
1604	Debates on the union in the English and Scottish Parliaments Royal Proclamation of Union
1606	Union flag designed
1606–7	Union debates dominated the second session of the English Parliament James successfully advanced the power of bishops in Scotland over presbyteries
1608	Colville's (Calvin's) case: the issue of naturalisation The case of the Post-nati
1610	The Courts of High Commision were restored in Scotland, consolidating the Crown's influence over the Church
1610	Scottish participation in the Plantation of Ulster
1611	Exile of Andrew Melville
1617	James's visit to Scotland
1618	Five Articles of Perth

The Union of England and Scotland is the first great panel under which the visitor stands on entering the Banqueting House. This union fulfilled James's destiny.

James VI of Scotland had a double claim to the English throne (see family tree). His mother was next in line to Elizabeth, descended from Henry VII of England, and his grandmother, the Countess of Lennox, passed her claim to

THE BRITISH SUCCESSION, 1603

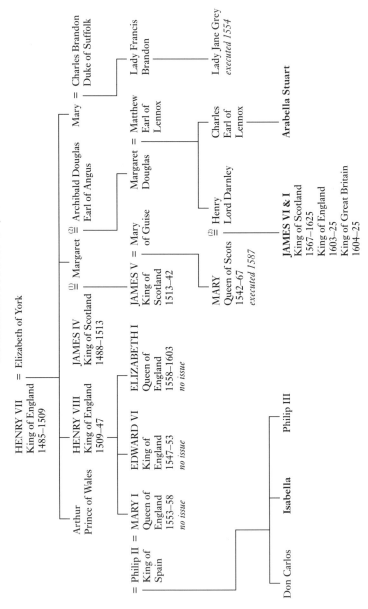

James on her death in 1578. On his mother's execution he is said to have declared 'I am now sole king.' Her death not only clarified his position in Scotland, but allowed him to prepare the way for succession to the English throne. In 1594 his son was christened Henry, not only an essentially English name, but the name of the king who had united the warring factions of Lancaster and York and founded a new dynasty as Henry VII, from whom he was lineally descended. His eldest daughter, born in 1596, was called Elizabeth as a gesture of respect to the English queen and godmother.

In the ideal world, James wanted a union encompassing one king, one faith, one language, one law, one parliament, one name, one flag. In the real world he was only too aware that union would bring problems that could not be glossed over by eloquence or the appeal to history, mythology or divine providence. He was no mere unionist windbag. Since his effective coming to power in Scotland he had had the British dimension in mind. From 1586 he was himself the leader of the English faction in Scotland; his handling of the demise of his mother [1.2, 1.3] was astute, and his attitude towards the Scottish Kirk shows clear evidence of a wish to bring about a degree of compromise between the Scottish and English Churches as a foundation of real union. His correspondence with Robert Cecil before his accession shows a sense of political realism and helped to bring about a very smooth succession to the southern kingdom on the death of Elizabeth in 1603.

The union raised deep issues of sovereignty, government, law, religion, commerce and nationality. It generated a great deal of debate in both the English and Scottish Parliaments as well as a host of tracts and historical inquiries. The question was not merely one of partial union or 'perfect union' but the myriad of meanings understood by these terms. Within these different goals the options were infinite as so many areas of vested interest were at stake. These issues have been extensively studied by Bruce Galloway; Gordon Donaldson has explored the Scottish dimension of the efforts; and Jenny Wormald has effectively integrated the Scottish and English aspects of his reign (see references at end of this chapter). James VI and I showed not only considerable eloquence in expressing his ideals, but good sense and restraint in handling the many frustrations to his schemes raised in his Parliaments, and ultimately wisdom in not pushing them beyond acceptability by recourse to prerogative measures.

The smooth change of dynasty produced a vast number of 'entertainments' celebrating the arrival of James and the union of Britain [2.1, 2.11]. James was keen to justify his succession and lay the foundations of union. Scottish and English Commissions were established to look into union and had completed an Instrument of Union for discussion by the Parliaments by 1604.

The major obstacles to union came from James's Parliaments, where the problems of the nature, extent and consequences of union were scrutinised [2.5, 2.7, 2.8, 2.13–2.21]. Regardless of exhortations from the king [2.2, 2.9, 2.18] and attempts to stress the fulfilment of British history through union [2.1, 2.2, 2.9, 2.11, 2.12], long-standing animosities urged caution [2.3, 2.4–2.8, 2.13, 2.21]. Union coinage was introduced [2.10], but like the idea of a union flag it lacked universal acceptance.

Ultimately 'perfect' union would rest on common institutions. The aim of one king was achieved, but the institutions supporting his authority in the two kingdoms remained separate. Union in Church, Law and Parliament never gained support and James I wisely chose a non-confrontational course. He settled for 'gradual' union after the second session of his first Westminster Parliament, following a policy of masterly inactivity. Although James's visit to Scotland in 1617 indicated his concern for maintaining and extending his authority there, the hostility that surrounded his attempted liturgical reforms in the Five Articles of Perth indicates a very uneasy Jacobean compromise in the Scottish Church.

King James's rule by the pen rather than the sword had merit. For the time being the acceptance of yet another foreign king in England and yet another absentee monarch in Scotland had little effect on the central institutions of both kingdoms. His vision of the union as something greater than a composite monarchy was sincere; Rubens has captured this in his ceiling panel [1.21] where James as Solomon ends the age-long hostilities between two mothers (England and Scotland) for the possession of a child (Great Britain). Union was far less than perfect; it was, however, far better than hostility.

Attitudes to union in 1603

2.1 The king's entertainment through the city of London, 1603–4

Great Monarch of the West, whose glorious stem
Doth now support a triple diadem,
Weighing more than that of thy grand-grandsire Brute,[1]
Thou that mayest make a King thy substitute,
And doest besides the red rose and the white,   5
With the rich flower of France thy garland dight,[2]
Wearing above Kings now, or those of old,
A double crown of laurel and of gold.

[1] Brute = Brutus, legendary founder of Britain after the Fall of Troy
[2] dight = decked, covered

J. Nichols, *The Progresses of James I*, vol. 1, 1828, p. 357

2.2 James I to the Commons, 19 March 1603/4[1]

Do we not yet remember, that this little Kingdom was divided into seven little kingdoms, besides Wales? And is it not now the stronger by their Union? And hath not the Union of Wales to England added a greater strength thereto? Which, tho' it was a great Principality, was nothing comparable, in greatness and power, to the ancient and famous Kingdom of Scotland ... Hath not God first united these Two   5
Kingdoms [Scotland and England] both in language, religion, and similitude of manners? Yea, hath he not made us all in one island, encompassed with one sea, and of itself by nature so indivisible, as almost those that were borderers themselves on the late borders, cannot distinguish, nor know or discern their own limits? These two countries being separated neither by sea nor by great river, mountain, nor the   10
strength of nature, but only by little small brooks, or demolished little walls; so as rather they were divided in apprehension, than in effect, and now, in the end and fullness of time, united, and right and title of both in My person alike lineally descended of both the Crowns ... What God hath conjoined then, let no man separate. I am the husband, and the whole isle is my lawful wife: I am the head,   15
and it is my body: I am the shepherd, and it is my flock ...

[1] During the seventeenth century the Julian Calendar was used in England. According to this the New Year began on 1 January, the time of the Roman festivities of Saturnalia. In medieval England the custom developed of beginning the New Year on the Feast of the Annunciation (25 March). Some writers give both years for dates between 1 January and 24 March.

J. R. Tanner, *Constitutional Documents of the Reign of James I, 1603–1625*, 1961, p. 26

Questions

1   Examine the family tree. Who were the possible claimants to the English throne in 1603? How strong were these claims?
2   Compare the justifications for union advanced in **2.1** and **2.2**.
3   How valid are these justifications? To what extent do they anticipate and resolve the fundamental problems of union?

Not everyone shared the idealism of **2.1** and **2.2**. The Venetian ambassador [**2.3**, **2.5**, **2.6**] records hostility and recalcitrance in 1603; the writer of **2.4** voices English vested interests.

2.3 Giovanni Carlo Scaramelli, Venetian secretary in London, to the doge and Senate, 4 June 1603

The ill-will between the English and Scottish goes on rising rapidly. It serves nothing that the King declares his resolve to extinguish both names, and that both people shall pass under the common name of Britons and be governed by one and the same law. The English, who were at first divided among themselves, begin now to make common cause against the Scots.

Calendar of State Papers Venetian, vol. 10, p. 44

2.4 Sir Henry Spelman's tract on union

To make SS [Scot] free of England, what will be the sequel? First many of their nobles and principal gentlemen will strive to creep themselves as near the Court as they can. And reason they should for who does not desire the influence of the prince. But our houses, our lands, our livings, shall be brought up in all places, the City and the country shall be replenished with SS: the Court shall abound with them. And   5
they having favour of the prince to beg and capacity by the laws to take, shall not only obtain leases and inheritances in all parts of England but the offices of state and government also. And whereas the Laws of England do not permit any alien nor denizen himself to bear any office of a constable, now by this Union the SS shall become capable of the high Constableship of England.

Bruce Galloway, *The Union of England and Scotland, 1603–1608*, 1986, p. 42

2.5 Giovanni Carlo Scaramelli, Venetian secretary in England, to the doge and Senate, 18 September 1603

Parliament is to deal with the question of the union of these two crowns, and to propose that both kingdoms should be united under the one name of Britain. The Scottish already let it be known that they will never consent to abandon their name, under which they have had down to the present one hundred and eight kings in the space of one thousand nine hundred and thirty-three years. They reckon from ...   5
three hundred and thirty years BC. They claim to preserve their ancient laws, and point to France as an instance of a kingdom possessing various codes.

Cal State Papers Venetian, vol. 10, p. 94

2.6 Giovanni Carlo Scaramelli, Venetian secretary in London, to the doge and Senate, 22 October 1603

After the Scottish courtiers returned to Scotland, very ill-pleased with the English, a meeting of Scottish nobles was summoned for the end of this month. It was to draw up a petition, and send it to the King by the hands of four leading nobles; they are to inform his Majesty that unless he grants the demands contained therein it will be impossible to effect the union of the two kingdoms and will endanger peace. The   5
chief points are that, as England fell by inheritance to the King of Scotland, England is to be considered accessory to Scotland; if that be impossible, then in case only one Council is to govern both kingdoms, the Scottish and English are to be equally represented in that Council, while each kingdom shall keep its own name and its own laws.

Cal State Papers Venetian, vol. 10, p. 106

Questions

1   What are the main issues of concern to the Scots in **2.5** and **2.6**?
2   How do the issues worrying the Scots in **2.5** and **2.6** differ in kind from those worrying Spelman in **2.4**?
3   Using the information from **2.3, 2.4, 2.5, 2.6** and your own knowledge, what were the main obstacles to union in 1603?

Issues of union in the Parliaments, 1604

James had proceeded in a very business-like way, allowing ample discussion by Commissions and Parliaments. In the English Commons he relied very heavily on Sir Francis Bacon. **2.7** consists of Bacon's analysis of objections to union and was reported to the Commons on 27 April 1604. Its full title was 'Objections against the change of the name or style of England and Scotland into the name or style of great Britanny; to be moved and debated in the Conference between the Lords and the Commons; and to that end by the Committees of the House of Commons collected, reviewed and reduced to order, for their better instruction'.

2.7 Sir Francis Bacon's collation of objections to the change in name

The matter of generality or common reason hath two parts:
That there is no cause of the change.
That there is no precedent of the like change.
The first objection therefore is:
That in ... any innovation or change, there ought to be either urgent necessity or   5
evident utility; but that we find no grief of our present estate, and foresee no
advancement to a better condition by this change ...
The second objection is:
That we find no precedent at home or abroad, of uniting or contracting of the names
of two several kingdoms of states into one name, where the union hath grown by   10
marriage or blood ...

Matter of estate inward, or matter of law, hath three main heads:

The first, that the alteration of the name of the King doth inevitably and infallibly
draw on the erection of a new kingdom or estate, and a dissolution ... of the old; and
that [any explanation] ... will be full of repugnancy and ambiguity, and subject to   15
much variety and danger of construction.

The second is ... a recital of ... confusions, incongruities, and mischiefs which will
necessarily and incidently follow in the time present; as
In the summoning of parliaments ...
In the seals of the kingdom: 20

In the great offices of the kingdom:
In the laws, customs, liberties and privileges of the kingdom:
In the residence and holding of such Courts as follow the King's person; which by
this generality of name may be held in Scotland:
In the several and reciprocal oaths: the one of his Majesty at his Coronation ... the   25
other, in the oaths of Allegiance, Homage, and Obedience, made and renewed from
time to time by the subjects.

All which acts, instruments and forms of policy and government, with a multitude of
other forms of Records, Writs, Pleadings and Instruments ... run now in the name of
England, and upon the change would be drawn into incertainty and question.   30

The matter of state foreign ... consisteth of three points:

The first is that Leagues, Treaties, foreign freedoms of trade and traffic ... may be
drawn into question ...

The second is that the King's precedence before other Christian kings, which is
guided by antiquity of kingdoms, and not by greatness, may be endangered, and his   35
place turned last, because it is the newest.

The third is that the glory and good acceptation of the English name and nation will
be, in foreign parts, obscured.

The matter of honour and reputation standeth upon four points:

The first is, no wordly thing is more dear to men than their name ...   40

The second is, that the contracted name of Britain will bring in oblivion the names of
England and Scotland.

The third is, that whereas now England, in the style, is placed before Scotland, in the
name of Britain that degree of priority or precedence will be lost.

The fourth is, that the change of name will be harsh in the popular opinion, and   45
unpleasing to the country.

Galloway, *The Union of England and Scotland*, 1986, appendix

2.8 Nicolo Molin, Venetian ambassador in England, to the doge and Senate, 28 April 1604

On Monday the question of the union of England and Scotland came up. The King
greatly desires it, but various difficulties arise; first, the Scottish claim the capacity to
hold all honours and dignities, which the English hold; the English are willing to
agree, but only on condition that the four great offices of Lord High Constable, Lord
Chancellor, Lord Keeper, and Lord Chamberlain shall always be held by the English,   5
and that no Scotsman may be appointed to any English office till the expiry of twelve
years ... The second difficulty is that the English insist that Scottish Peers shall not
rank in England, while the Scots claim equal rank for their peerage with that of
English, and that seniority of patent alone should count. The third difficulty is that
the English claim that Scotland shall be taxed as England is taxed ... On the other   10

hand the Scottish plead their poverty and declare that they cannot pay a penny more than their present charges. These points are sustained and argued by both sides with such heat that the King doubts whether he will be able to surmount the difficulties.

Cal State Papers Venetian, vol. 10, p. 148

Questions

1 Which of Bacon's objections [2.7] do you consider to be the most valid, and why?
2 How might you answer the objections that:
  (i) there was no cause for change
  (ii) law and government would suffer confusion
  (iii) England would lose status abroad
  (iv) the honour of England would suffer from a change in name?
3 How far does the evidence of 2.8 support the fears expressed in the objections?

With both Parliaments dragging their heels over union and such matters as the royal style, James resorted to the device of Proclamation to change the style and introduce coins for the whole island bearing the names 'Unite' and 'Britain's Crowne' on which were displayed his new title 'King of Britain, France and Ireland'. The coinage was a practical as well as a cosmetic measure: £12 Scots was equivalent to £1 Sterling.

2.9 Proclamation by James I, 20 October 1604

Wherefore we have thought good to discontinue the divided names of England and Scotland out of our regal Style, and do intend and resolve to take and assume unto Us in manner and form hereafter expressed, the name and Style of King of Great Britain, including therein according to the truth, the whole Island. Wherein no man can imagine Us to be led by an humour of vainglory or ambition, because we should   5 in that case, rather delight in a long enumeration of many Kingdoms ... Nor that We covet any new affected Name devised at Our pleasure, but out of undoubted knowledge do use the true and ancient name, which God and Time have imposed upon this Isle ... and received in Histories, in all Maps and Charts ... in Letters ... from foreign Princes ... and warranted by charters ... and other Records of great   10 Antiquity, giving us precedent for our doing, not borrowed out of foreign nations, but from the Acts of our progenitors, Kings of this realm of England, both before and since the Conquest, having not had so just and great cause as We have.

Upon which considerations We do by these Presents, by force of our Kingly Power and prerogative, assume to Our self by the clearness of our right, the Name and Style   15

of **KING OF GREAT BRITAIN, FRANCE, AND IRELAND, DEFENDER OF THE FAITH,**
etc. … And do hereby publish, promulgate and declare the same, to the end that in
all Proclamations, Missives foreign and domestical, treaties, leagues, Dedicatories,
Impressions, and in all other cases of like nature, the same may be used and
observed. And to the end the same may be the sooner and more universally divulged   20
both at Home and abroad: Our will and pleasure is that the same Style be from
henceforth used upon our current Moneys and Coins of gold and silver hereafter to
be minted …

***Stuart Royal Proclamations, Royal Proclamations of King James I, 1603–1625,*
1973, ed. J. F Larking and P. L. Hughes, vol. 1, pp. 94–97**

2.10 Unite coins issued by James I

Questions

1   What is a Royal Proclamation? Why did James have recourse to this
    method of changing his regal style and coinage?
2   How does James justify his new style in the Proclamation?
3   How significant were such features as style and coinage in achieving the
    union of the two kingdoms?

The importance of a name

Sources **2.11** and **2.12** show the continuing interest in the name and style that
James wished to be known by. The blatant confusion of history and legend
puts them in the genre of medieval chronicles but James obviously approved
of such dynastic toadying.

The Lyte Pedigree [2.12] brought a handsome reward for its designer – a Hilliard miniature of James I. While the pedigree emphasises the importance of the 'British' theme to James, the significance of this should not be exaggerated. While the 'British' inheritance rationalised James's accession, the presentation of a pedigree should be seen in the common tradition of the pedigree of Elizabeth at Hatfield House, where her origins are traced back to Adam. (Even further back in time, all good Anglo-Saxon kings claimed Woden as an ancestor!)

2.11 An entertainment on the triumphs of reunited Britannia by A. Mundy, citizen and draper of London, and performed for the inauguration of the Lord Mayor of London in 1605

Most writers do agree that after the deluge Noah was the sole monarch of all the world, and he divided the dominion of the whole earth to his three sons: all Europe with the isles ... fell to Japhet ... Samothes, the sixth son of Japhet [was] the first King over ... the Celts and Britons, who were then ... called Samotheans ...

Thus continued the name of Samothes the space of 310 years, till Neptune put his   5
son Albion, the giant, in possession of this land ... who called this island Albion ...

The country thus peopled with giants, and continuing after the name of Albion for 600 years: Brute ... with the remains of Troyan followers, arrived and landed at Totnes ...

Brute having the whole land in his own quiet possession, began to build a City, near   10
the side of the river Thames ... which he named Troynovant, or ... New Troy. Now began he to alter the name of the island, and according to his own name, called it Britain, and caused all the inhabitants to be named Britons ...

After Brute, I find not any other alteration of our country's name, until the reign of King Egbert, who about the year of grace 800, and the first of his reign, gave a   15
special edict, dated at Winchester; that it should be named Angles Land ... which we do pronounce England ...

And, what fierce war by no means could effect,
To re-unite those sundered lands in one;
The hand of Heaven did peacefully elect,   20
By mildest grace, to seat on Britain's throne
This second Brute, than whom there else was none.
Wales, England, Scotland, severed first by me,
To knit again in blessed unity.

Nichols, *The Progresses of James I* , 1828, vol. 1, pp. 564ff.

2.12 The Lyte Pedigree

2.12 (a) Sir Thomas Lyte, *The Lyte Pedigree*, *c.* 1605–10, tracing the descent of James I from Brutus

2.12(b) A miniature by Nicholas Hilliard given to Thomas Lyte in 1610 as a reward for his genealogy tracing James back to Brutus

Religion and the union

While the literary and artistic celebration of union continued, effective union was proving elusive [2.13, 2.14]. In Scotland James had long followed a policy of trying to bring the Scottish Church somewhat in line with the English by favouring bishops. Andrew Melville and six Scottish Presbyterian ministers were invited to London to discuss common ground; negotiations failed, resulting in the imprisonment and subsequent exile of Melville, whose intransigence on liturgy and episcopal ordination had led him to denounce Archbishop Bancroft's lawn sleeves – the sleeves of fine linen that bishops wore – as 'Romish rags'. It was a further source of frustration for James that the hostile laws[1] had not yet been repealed, but the most hotly debated issues of union in the First Parliament were those of naturalisation [**2.15–2.17, 2.21**] and the nature of the union [**2.18**].

2.13 Zorzi Giustinian, Venetian ambassador in England, to the doge and Senate, 11 October 1606

The conference between the Scottish Ministers and English Bishops has begun. Its object is the unification of rites, but the Scotch display violent opposition and refuse to attend the sermons which the King has ordered. This augurs ill for the question of union between the Kingdoms, which is to be raised in the coming Parliament; for without union of Churches, union of Kingdoms is thought impossible.

Cal State Papers Venetian, vol. 10, p. 411

Union debates in the second session of the First Parliament

There is no doubt that the issue of union was of fundamental importance to both James and his Parliaments in England and Scotland. Anti-Scottish speeches in 1607 by the xenophobic Sir Christopher Pigott, the MP for Buckinghamshire, did not help; he referred to the Scots as 'murderers, thieves and rogues' who 'have not suffered above two Kings to die in their beds these 200 years; our King hath hardly escaped them; they have attempted him'. It is interesting to speculate whether the Scots were more angry at the insults of this maverick than they were at an English MP's appropriation of a Scottish king! James was at his best in smoothing over differences in a letter to the Scottish Privy Council [**2.16**].

2.14 The opening of Parliament, 18 November 1606

Then the King's Majesty used an eloquent and very long speech which continued an hour and half; the chief and almost only effect whereof was, to persuade the passage of the Act and Instrument of Union ... The chiefest argument which his Highness used was, that this happy Union is already in his Person made by the Singular Providence of God; that now it only remaineth that the same be confirmed by the   5 Parliament, so as no splinter may start out; which principally will be by abolishing all the old former Laws of Hostility.

The Parliamentary Diary of Robert Bowyer, 1606–1607, ed. D. H. Willson, 1931, p. 185

[1] Border or 'hostile' laws, a great rag-bag of customs and local laws (of Scottish or English origin) which had arisen over the centuries to deal with everyday problems peculiar to the border regions, for example problems of jurisdiction, cross-border theft, hot pursuit and enforcing payment.

2.15 Report of Sir Edwyn Sandys to the Commons, 7 March 1606/7

Sir Edwyn Sandys reported, that the Committees for this great Conference touching naturalization had met ... but the business in itself to be so large, that they could not go through the whole ... A second point debated by the Committees was whether the word Naturalization shall be used in the Conference, for that the Lawyers thought a new word, and therefore not determinable in seven years ...

Willson, *The Parliamentary Diary*, pp. 219ff.

2.16 Letter of James VI to the Scottish Privy Council explaining the circumstances of Pigott's derogatory speech against the Scots, sent from Royston on 17 March 1607

But, as the common proverb goeth, 'The devil is not so black as he is called'; so these speeches of Pigott were not altogether so hard as they have been reported or advertised unto you. And, albeit there was more than most sufficient cause both to take exception and to be offended with them, yet not only in the beginning, but also in the end thereof, he made special declaration that his meaning in those speeches   5
was not against that whole nation, but only against that sort of people therein, who either had never been under obedience, or than such as had their blood stained with the detestable blot of treason. And, indeed, among such a number as in that House were then gathered it is neither wonder nor novelty to see some persons perhaps of small discretion and distempered humour. But, howsoever the report of those   10
speeches might have come to you, yet the taciturnity of the rest of that House and that he was not presently answered is by you very far mistaken, and your informers therein have wronged them much; for that proceded of nothing else but their amazement and wondering at the indiscretion of the party.

Register of the Privy Council of Scotland, ed. D. Masson, vol. 7, *1604–1607*, 1885, p. 517

2.17 Zorzi Giustinian, Venetian ambassador in England, to the doge and Senate, 29 March 1607

Parliament is discussing the naturalization of the Post-nati. This motion if carried would in the course of a few years produce the Union automatically. This is violently opposed by those who do not desire the Union. The King complains bitterly that his advisers, by representing the achievement of the Union as an easy affair, have committed him to a labyrinth, in which his honour is involved. Two evils are   5
indicated, one the revival of the ancient enmity between the two countries, the other the growth of Parliamentary as opposed to Royal authority.

Cal State Papers Venetian, vol. 10, p. 485

2.18 King James I adjourning Parliament, 31 March 1607

I desire a perfect Union of Laws and persons, and such a Naturalizing as may make
one body of both Kingdoms under me your King, that I and my posterity (if it so
please God) may rule over you to the world's end; such an Union as was of the Scots
and Picts in Scotland, and of the Heptarchy here in England. And for Scotland I
avow such an Union, as if you had got it by Conquest, but such a Conquest as may be   5
cemented by love, the only sure bond of subjection or friendship; that as there is over
both but unus Rex, so there may be in both but unus Grex & una Lex[1]: For no more
possible is it for one King to govern two Countries *contiguous*, the one a great, the
other a less, a richer and a poorer, the greater drawing like an Adamant[2] the lesser to
the Commodities thereof, than for one head to govern two bodies, or one man to be   10
the husband of two wives …

… For when I speak of a perfect Union, I mean not confusion of all things: you must
not take from Scotland those particular Privileges that may stand as well with this
Union, as in England many particular customs in particular shires … do with the
Common Law of the Kingdom … But I mean of such a general Union of Laws as   15
may reduce the whole Island, that as they live already under one Monarch, so they
may be governed by one Law … I desire not the abolishing of the Laws, but only the
clearing and sweeping off the rust of them, and that by Parliament our Laws might
be cleared and made known to all subjects … And now may you have fair occasion of
amending and polishing your Laws, when Scotland is to be united with you under   20
them …

But this is not possible to be done without a fit preparation … and that was my end
in causing the Instrument of Union to be made …

[I am misjudged in a number of things.] First, that this Union will be the *Crisis* to the
overthrow of England and setting up of Scotland …   25

The second is, my profuse liberality to the Scottish men more than the English, and
that with this Union all things shall be given to them, and you turned out of all …

Some think that I will draw the Scottish Nation hither, talking idly of transporting of
Trees out of a barren ground into a better, and of lean cattle out of bad pasture into a
more fertile soil …   30

For the manner of the Union presently desired, It standeth in 3 parts: The first,
taking away of hostile Laws … The second is community of Commerce … For the
third point, of Naturalization, All you agree that they are no Aliens, and yet will
not allow them to be natural … But for the Post-nati, your own Lawyers and Judges
at my first coming to this Crown, informed me, there was a difference between   35
the Ante and the Post-nati of each Kingdom, which caused me to publish a
Proclamation, that the Post-nati of each Kingdom were naturalized (Ipso facto)
by my accession to this Crown …

And for the point of Naturalizing … I will maintain two principles … The one, that
it is a special point of the King's own Prerogative, to make aliens citizens … The   40
other, that in any case wherein the Law is thought not to be clear … then in such a

question wherein no positive Law is resolute, Rex est Iudex,[3] for he is Lex loquens.[4]

This I must say for Scotland, and I may truly vaunt it; here I sit, and govern it with my Pen; I write, and it is done; and by a Clerk of the Council I govern Scotland now, which others could not do by the Sword. And for their averseness in their heart   45 against the Union; it is true indeed ... they did never crave this Union of me ... but on the other part, they offered always to obey me, when it should come to them ... I know that there are amongst them ... a number of seditious and discontented particular persons ... but no Scottishmen ever spake dishonourable of England in Parliament.

[1] unus Rex = one king; unus Grex = one flock [people]; una Lex = one law
[2] Adamant = magnet
[3] Rex est Iudex = the king is the judge
[4] Lex loquens = the law speaking

Political Works of James I, ed. C. H. McIlwain, 1918, pp. 290ff.

2.19 Mr Fuller's reply to Sir Edwyn Sandys, 29 April 1607

There is benefit say some by this Union; it is true, but the whole benefit is to the other side; for I do not hear of any English preferred there; therefore the profit is theirs; let them first make their Law for this Union, and let not us begin ... Yet let us do somewhat, let us make a law forthwith to abolish Hostile Laws, and this not by Conference, but by Bill ...

Willson, *The Parliamentary Diary*, pp. 263–64

2.20 Zorzi Giustinian, Venetian ambassador in England, to the doge and Senate, 29 March 1607

The Duke of Lennox has arrived and has informed the King that he has dismissed the Scottish Parliament from which he had obtained the confirmation of everything that the English Parliament had decided, and he further promises that as far as the Scottish are concerned his Majesty will never be cheated of his wish in this matter. Though the King is pleased, his pleasure is outweighed by his displeasure that the   5 same Parliament has refused to grant two of his requests ... the first was his claim to the headship of the Scottish Kirk ... the other point was the privileges of peers; for in Scotland the privileges are far greater than in England and the Scottish will not submit to any diminution of the same. Both points are of such importance to the question of Union that unless they are settled the Union can never take place, and   10 so it is no wonder that their rejection has greatly disturbed the King.

Cal State Papers Venetian, vol. 10, p. 485

2.21 Marc Antonion Correr, Venetian ambassador in England, to the doge and Senate, 1 April 1610

There is no talk of the Union, only some ten Scotch gentlemen have been naturalized; and as there is discovered great difficulty in the way of the Union, they intend to leave the matter to ripen by time and to become familiar by the inter-marriage of the two races, by a gradual naturalization through graces, and by the doctrine that all children born after the King's accession to the throne are ipso facto   5 admissible to the privileges of both Kingdoms. On this subject the King consulted the Doctors in Common Law, who, all save one, favoured his Majesty's design.

Cal State Papers Venetian, vol. 11, p. 12

There is an argument for saying that the lengthy debates suited both the English and Scots and frustrated James. Ultimately the Parliaments repealed the hostile laws and, as we have seen already, James used proclamation to alter his style and introduce new coins. The union flag for ships was rarely used, the question of union of parliaments was never debated, that of legal union proved sterile, and the Presbyterian Scottish Church retained its independence of the Archbishop of Canterbury. The Scots gained little in commerce; by 1610 the same customs were levied on Anglo-Scottish trade as on Anglo-Irish trade, although the Scots obviously benefited by the opportunity to settle in Ulster with James's Plantation.

James persisted with the question of naturalisation. He deliberately used the English courts to achieve the naturalisation of the Post-nati in the collusive case known as Calvin's case or Colville's case. Two English estates were conveyed to a Scot born after 1603 – the three-year-old Robert Colville, grandchild of Lord Colville (also referred to as Colvyn and anglicised as Calvin). The lands were then seized and a case brought on behalf of the young plaintiff against defendants who would insist that the plaintiff, as an alien, was unfit to plead. One case was heard in King's Bench, the other in Chancery. Both went to the Court of the Exchequer Chamber for reference. The case for the plaintiff, Colville, was put by Bacon and Hobart, Bacon stressing the fundamental loyalty of the subject to the person of the king, who could create a denizen by letters patent. The defence case rested on allegiance belonging to the king's 'body politic' (i.e. kingdom rather than his 'natural' body). According to Bruce Galloway (see recommended reading), fourteen judges from King's Bench and Common Pleas, together with the Exchequer barons and the Lord Chancellor, heard the case. The majority (12:2) decided in favour of the plaintiff, Colville. This established the precedent desired by the king for recognition of the legal status of the Post-nati in a way much less fraught than statutory recognition.

Questions

1 Explain the meaning and significance of the terms Post-nati and Ante-nati.
2 What were the key issues at stake in the question of naturalisation?
3 How would you argue that the demands for perfect union were merely delaying devices for any union?
4 To what extent was the authority of James challenged by the issue of the Post-nati?
5 In what ways and to what extent do you find James's arguments for union in **2.18** stronger than his earlier statements on the matter?

The question of union in lower profile

The visit to Scotland by the king in 1617 was less than successful. Adulatory addresses were poured out to him from the royal burghs, but his attempts to align the liturgies of the two countries by the Five Articles of Perth (1618) threatened the stability of his control over religion in Scotland not only by their content, which required observance of holy days and kneeling at communion, but by the manner in which they were pushed through a packed Scottish Parliament in 1621. It was clear that James saw religious integration as a prerequisite to union; while he was prepared to send the inflexible William Laud back to England lest he disturb the situation in Scotland, James himself was not prepared to abandon the closer relationship between the two national Churches that he had been designing for years before the acquisition of the southern kingdom.

The deep suspicion that Scots were influencing the king to the detriment of English courtiers has been a theme in a number of extracts. Court patronage was jealously sought and anti-Scottish prejudice assiduously fostered as a form of self-defence. Few, however, went to the lengths of Weldon. His piece shows extreme bad taste; what it stands for illustrates the difficulties James faced in reconciling vested interests in both kingdoms.

2.22 A description of Scotland by Sir Anthony Weldon, 1617

First, for the Country I must confess it is too good for those that possess it, and too bad for others to be at the charge to conquer it. The air might be wholesome but for the stinking people that inhabit it, the ground might be fruitful had they the will to manure it. Their beasts be generally small, women only excepted, of which sort there are none greater in all the world. There is great store of fowl, as foul houses, foul sheets and shirts, foul linen, foul dishes and pots, foul trenchers and napkins ... 5
They have likewise great store of deer ... [but] I confess all the deer I met withal was

dear lodgings, dear horse-meat, dear tobacco and English beer ... The thistle was not given them of naught, for it is the fairest flower in their garden ... They christen without the cross, marry without the ring, receive the sacrament without reverence,   10 die without repentance, and bury without divine service ... They keep no holy days, nor acknowledge no Saint but St Andrew, who, they say, got that honour by presenting Christ with an oaten cake after his forty days' fast ... The country, although it be mountainous, affords no monsters but women ... To be chained in marriage with one of them were as to be tied to a dead carcase and cast into a stinking   15 ditch ...

And therefore, to conclude, the men of old did no more wonder that the great Messias should be born in so poor a town as Bethlem in Judea, as I do wonder that so brave a Prince as King James should be borne in so stinking a town as Edinburgh in 1—sy Scotland.

Nichols, *The Progresses of King James I*, vol. 3, 1828, pp. 338–43

Questions

1   How far do you agree that James's success in Calvin's case was the foundation to a gradual union?
2   How seriously did the prejudices indicated in **2.22** work against union?
3   Consider the view that **2.22** reflects worse on its author than it does on Scotland.
4   In spite of xenophobia on both sides, what progress had been made in union by the end of the reign of James I?

Recommended reading

K. M. Brown, *Kingdom or Province? Scotland and the Regal Union, 1603–1715*, 1992
D. Daiches, *Scotland and the Union*, 1977
G. Donaldson, *Scotland James V–James VII*, 1990
W. Ferguson, *Scotland's Relations with England, A Survey to 1707*, 1977
B. Galloway, *The Union of England and Scotland 1603–1608*, 1986
A. H. Williamson, *Scottish National Consciousness in the Age of James VI*, 1979
D. H. Willson (ed.), *The Parliamentary Diary of Robert Bowyer, 1606–1607*, 1931
J. Wormald, *Court, Kirk and Community, Scotland 1470–1625*, 1981
J. Wormald, 'James VI and I: two kings or one?', *History*, vol. 68, 1983

3 'The Jacobean compromise' James I and religion

Time chart	
1603	Millenary Petition
	Bye Plot
	Main Plot
1604	Hampton Court Conference
	Proclamation enjoining conformity
	Bancroft's Canons
1605	Gunpowder Plot
1606	Oath of Allegiance
1610	Death of Bancroft and elevation of Abbot to Canterbury
1611	Exile of Andrew Melville
	Authorized Version of the Bible
1617	Visit of James to Scotland
1618	Five Articles of Perth
	Declaration on Sports
	Outbreak of the Thirty Years War
	Synod of Dort
1621	Pressure for a more active foreign policy in aid of Protestants
1624	Hostility to Arminians voiced in the 1624 Parliament

It is difficult for citizens of a modern pluralist society to appreciate the political and social significance of religion in the early seventeenth century. The *cuius regio, eius religio* principle – that each state be required to follow the religion of its leader – had emerged in the Peace of Augsburg of 1555, which settled the religious wars in Germany. It gained wider implicit currency in Europe, and religious conformity became an essential demonstration of loyalty to the head of state. Religious deviance was tantamount to treason in an age where Reformation and Counter Reformation were still powerful dynamics.

48

The first King of Great Britain appreciated the importance of religious conformity and the need to exercise control over the power of the pulpit, but without a British Church as such, he faced the intractable problem of a composite arrangement with one king and separate religious traditions. Religious uniformity throughout the three kingdoms proved elusive; for the most part a policy of cautious compromise was pursued.

In England and Wales, conformity to the Church of England both symbolised loyalty and provided the head of state with a hierarchic bureaucracy that was to a greater or lesser extent inherited from that most structured of all bureaucracies, the Roman Catholic Church. While the pope was rejected during the English Reformation in the reign of Henry VIII (1509–47), archbishops, bishops, archdeacons, deans and parish clergy remained, with the sovereign as supreme governor. Henry's successor, Edward VI (1547–53), moved towards a more Protestant Church of England; this process was interrupted by his death and the succession of his Roman Catholic half-sister, Mary (1553–58), and the attempted restoration of the Roman Catholic Church in England. This religious instability was eased by the accession of Elizabeth (1558–1603), who pursued a religious compromise, a *via media* or middle way: in her own words, 'I will not animate Romanism; neither will I tolerate Newfangledness.' Her compromise between Rome and Geneva stressed a Church of England 'as by law established' with the monarch as 'supreme governor in things as well spiritual as temporal'. The Acts of Uniformity and Supremacy of 1559 together with the Thirty-Nine Articles of Faith formed the basis of the Elizabethan Settlement, to which all subjects had to conform. This broad-based conformity was both a strength and weakness of the Church of England by the end of the reign of Elizabeth. The compromise became increasingly difficult to maintain as religious differences between the High and Low Church groups were sharpened by the growth of Puritanism at home, and Arminianism and religious wars abroad. The fundamental nature of the English Church was in question: was it a reformed Catholic Church, acknowledging its origins and episcopal authority as stemming from the Church of Rome, or was it a reformed Church to which Rome was Anti-Christ and the Whore of Babylon, every single vestige of which should be eradicated from the Church of England?

The overriding interests of James I in religion were those of unity, loyalty and conformity [3.6–3.9]. The structure of the Church of England, firmly rooted in parish and diocese, offered a chain of communication from the sovereign at Whitehall through the diocesan bishops to the parish laity, a captive audience in an age of compulsory religious attendance. The role of the sovereign within the Church was ideally suited to James's theory of the Divine

Right of Kings. As supreme governor, James could exercise the royal prerogative over the Church. His support of the bishops, whose authority was also divine in origin, never wavered. He promoted learned men to the bench of bishops and understood only too well the importance of his statement at the Hampton Court Conference, 'No Bishop, no King' [3.4].

James was aware of the dangers to the Church of England from Puritans [3.1–3.10] and Roman Catholics [3.11–3.23]. The former were difficult to target as they were for the most part within the Church of England rather than Separatists (those who separated from the Church of England); they sought to strengthen the Calvinist elements of the Church in both doctrine and liturgy [3.1, 3.10]. His dealings with them produced the debates at Hampton Court in 1604 as a response to the Millenary Petition of 1603 [3.1], a tighter definition of clerical conformity by Bancroft's Canons [3.8], some hostility over the Declaration on Sports [3.27], and considerable Puritan anxiety at the direction of his foreign policy after 1618 [6.10, 6.11]. The Roman Catholics made a more coherent target. Ever since the Papal Bull of 1570 which excommunicated Queen Elizabeth, Roman Catholics were by definition traitors to the Crown; the pope's claimed right to depose excommunicated sovereigns was feared. Harsh penal laws restricted Roman Catholics, and recusancy fines could be imposed on those who failed to attend the Church of England [3.23]. While James preferred not to alienate Roman Catholics, his hand was forced by plots which triggered the anti-Catholic reaction early on in his reign. These include the Bye Plot (an attempt by the secular priest Fr William Watson, to capture James and make him grant religious toleration for Roman Catholics), the Main Plot (involving Lord Cobham and Sir Walter Raleigh) and the Gunpowder Plot of 1605. It is suggested that the early plots involved the removal of James in favour of a Spanish Catholic candidate, the Infanta Isabella (who demonstrated no interest in such schemes). Jenny Wormald has linked the Gunpowder Plotters with English Catholic pro-Spanish and anti-Scottish feeling. Their substitute for James was not the Infanta Isabella but James's nine-year-old daughter, the Princess Elizabeth. They represented a group of disgruntled Roman Catholic gentry, many in the Midland shires, prepared to take a great leap into the dark by removing the Protestant establishment with its Scottish parasites. Ever the man of reason and compromise, James hoped that the Oath of Allegiance [3.21] might achieve a *modus vivendi*. In this he was disappointed [3.22]. Apart from the plots, the paranoid fears of English subjugation to Spain at the end of the reign as a result of the Spanish marriage scheme, and a persistently strong Catholic presence at court illustrated by the conversion of the queen and the vogue for such conversions in the early 1620s, meant that English Catholicism was always an issue of great complexity.

A degree of polarisation could be seen in the Church of England by 1625. James's Jacobean compromise wore thin under the pressure of events in Europe such as the Dutch Synod of Dort (1618–19) and the outbreak of the Thirty Years War. The former was convened to deal with the Arminian Controversy. The followers of Arminius stressed free will or choice in acceptance of grace and salvation rather than the traditional Calvinist belief in double predestination which divided the world into the elect (the saved) and the reprobate (the damned) regardless of their own choice or effort. James opted for an anti-Arminian stand by the English delegates but urged his clergy at home not to encourage popular debate on such matters as predestination and free will. Early in his reign the so-called English Arminians had been learned clergy such as Richard Neile, Lancelot Andrews, John Cosin, Richard Montague and William Laud. They stressed the Catholic tradition of the Church of England, the importance of bishops, and what came to be known as 'the beauty of holiness'. While James remained a good Calvinist in his attitude towards predestination and in his support for the orthodox Calvinist stand at Dort, he promoted Arminians not because they were active advocates of free will but because they were scholarly, diligent and able men in their dioceses. Tyacke sees James as more amenable to the Arminians at the end of his reign. He knew that he could rely on their support of his authority in both Church and State. Fincham believes that James's attitude towards Arminians in England was motivated by the need for the balance of extremes within the Church of England. There is, however, no doubt that by the end of the reign Arminianism had become a political issue. Its rise was complained of in Parliament by John Pym in 1624. This was to some extent a product of the Puritan reaction to the Thirty Years War: the success of the Catholic powers was resented, and English high church men were castigated as Arminians, defined by Francis Rous in 1626 as a 'spawn of the papist', undermining the English Reformation and State by associations with the Jesuits, the pope and the King of Spain [3.29]. Religious divisions in England had certainly sharpened in the reign of James, generating a religious sensitivity that made any gradual evolution of a British Church even less likely than it had been in 1603.

Constant and central to James's religious thinking was a Calvinist outlook derived from his upbringing at the height of the Scottish Reformation when government by bishops was largely replaced by the Presbyterian system. The word 'Presbyterian' is derived from the Greek *presbuteros*, meaning 'elder'; in this system presbyteries (bodies of ministers and elders, equal in rank) supervised groups of parishes. James lacked the institutionalised authority over the Presbyterian Church that he was to enjoy over the Church of England: the leading Scottish reformer, Andrew Melville, had asserted that only Christ was

'King and Head of the Church'; some bishops did remain in the Presbyterian system but their authority was subject to the General Assembly. Throughout his reign James strove to prevent the elimination of bishops in Scotland and to strengthen their authority together with his own. This met with the dour opposition of Melville, which led to his exile in 1611. The king's visit to Scotland in 1617 culminated in the Five Articles of Perth, James's attempt in 1618 to align the liturgies of England and Scotland. They encountered passive resistance, and their strict enforcement certainly proved alienatory. In short he made little real progress towards religious unity on a British scale. The theme of his work in both kingdoms was compromise. Both countries had Roman Catholic minorities, both had groups demanding further reform, and in both the position of the authority of the Crown in Church affairs was a key issue.

The ultimate Jacobean compromise in religion was achieved by default in Ireland. The native population was overwhelmingly Roman Catholic. The descendants of the pre-Reformation English settlers (the Old English) were mainly Roman Catholic. The New English (post-Reformation English settlers) were Protestant members of the established Church of Ireland (the Church of England in Ireland). To this James added Scottish Presbyterian settlers in the Ulster Plantation of 1610. While overall lip service was paid to the Church of Ireland, it was a weak Church and the religious situation in Ireland remained confused.

The Puritan problem and the British Solomon

The major problem for James in 1603 was the demand from certain clergy within the Church of England, as expressed within the Millenary Petition, 'for reformation of certain ceremonies and abuses of the Church'.

3.1 The Millenary Petition, 1603

Most gracious and dread sovereign, seeing it hath pleased the Divine Majesty ... to advance your Highness according to your just title, to the peaceable government of this church and Commonwealth of England; we the ministers of the gospel in this land, neither as factious men affecting a popular parity in the Church, nor as schismatics aiming at the dissolution of the state ecclesiastical; but as the faithful   5
servants of Christ, and loyal subjects to your Majesty, desiring and longing for the redress of divers abuses of the Church, could do no less ... than acquaint your princely Majesty with our particular griefs. For, as your princely pen writeth: 'The king, as a good physician, must first know what peccant humours his patient naturally is most subject unto, before he can begin his cure' ... Now we, to the   10
number of more than a thousand, of your Majesty's subjects and ministers, all groaning as under a common burden of human rites and ceremonies ... do humble

ourselves at your Majesty's feet to be eased and relieved in this behalf. Our humble suit, then, unto your Majesty is, that [of] these offences following, some may be removed, some amended, some qualified: 15

I *In the church-service* That the cross in baptism, interrogatories ministered to infants, confirmation, as superfluous, may be taken away: baptism not to be ministered by women, and so explained: the cap and surplice not urged: that examination may go before the communion; that it be ministered with a sermon; that divers terms of priests and absolution, and some others used, with the ring in   20 marriage, and other such like in the Book, may be corrected: the longsomeness of service abridged: church-songs and music moderated to better edification: that the Lord's Day be not profaned, the rest upon holy-days not so strictly urged: that there may be a uniformity of doctrine prescribed: no popish opinion to be any more taught or defended: no ministers charged to teach their people to bow at the   25 name of Jesus: that the canonical scripture only be read in the church.

II *Concerning church ministers* That none hereafter be admitted into the ministry but able and sufficient men; and those to preach diligently, and especially upon the Lord's day ...

III *For church livings and maintenance* That bishops leave their commendams[1]... that   30 double-beneficed men[2] be not suffered to hold some two, some three, benefices with cure,[3] and some two, three, or four dignities besides ...

IV *For church discipline* That the discipline and excommunication may be administered according to Christ's own institution ...

These ... we are able to show not to be agreeable to the scriptures, if it shall please   35 your Highness farther to hear us ... or by conference among the learned to be resolved ... God, we trust, hath appointed your Highness our physician to heal these diseases ...

Your Majesty's most humble subjects, the ministers of the gospel, that desire not a disorderly innovation, but a due and godly reformation.

[1] commendams = benefices which a bishop or other church dignitary held together with his see
[2] double-beneficed = clergy who held more than one benefice (rectory, vicarage or curacy)
[3] cure = a clergyman with 'cure of souls' had charge of a parish

Fuller, *Church History*, vol. 3, pp. 215–17, quoted in J. P. Kenyon, *The Stuart Constitution*, 1966, p. 132

Questions

1 What, according to the Millenary Petitioners, were the main abuses in the Church of England in 1603?
2. What devices of tone and style are used within the Petition to elicit a favourable response from James?
3 To what extent is there justification for regarding this Petition as a statement of Puritan objectives and policy in 1603?

James took this petition seriously for a number of reasons. He was keen to appear wise and attentive to religious issues. Above all, he was keen to assert his authority over the Church. This is very clearly indicated in the following extract, in which the Venetian ambassador considers the position of the group at the other end of the spectrum in 1603, the Roman Catholics.

3.2 Giovanni Carlo Scaramelli, Venetian secretary in England, to the doge and Senate, 28 May 1603

The King is convinced that the security and peace of the kingdom depend upon the question of religion, and has resolved, in order to put an end to all doubts, to declare himself head and governor of the Anglican Church, although in the proclamation of Accession he was purposely not called such. He proposes to exact the oath from all servants of the Crown, even if they are Catholics, declare that God has touched their hearts, and that the example of their king has more weight with them than the disputes of theologians. They have become Protestants, and go to Church in the train of the King. He declares that he does not want the recusants[1] to pay money for not going, but wishes all to go in the same spirit as he goes.

5

[1] recusants = Roman Catholics who refused to attend the Church of England and after 1581 paid recusancy fines of £20 per month

Calendar of State Papers Venetian, vol. 10, p. 39

3.3 A response to the Millenary Petition

We have observed two contrary factions, that have shown themselves by their Petitions, discontented with the present State and Ecclesiastical Government: namely in the Papists and the Puritans … Verily these men are like Samson's foxes.[1] They have their heads severed indeed, the one sort looking to the Papacy, the other to the Presbytery. But they are tied together by the tails, with firebrands between them. Which if they be not quenched in time; are able to set the whole land in a combustion and uproar.

5

[1] Samson's foxes = the three hundred foxes caught by Samson – he tied torches between their tails and then set them to burn the crops of the Philistines (Judges 15).

The Answer of the Vice Chancellor, the Doctors, both Proctors, and the Other Heads of the Houses in the University of Oxford etc. to the Humble Petition of the Ministers of the Church of England, desiring Reformation of Certain Ceremonies and Abuses of the Church, dedicated to the Archbishop of Canterbury, Lord Buckhurst, Lord Cecil and the Privy Council, **Oxford, 1603 (British Library Tract)**

Questions

1 In the light of the evidence in **3.1** and **3.2**, how justified are the fears expressed by the writers of **3.3**?
2 How do the writers of **3.3** use language and style to emphasise their attitude to Church reform?
3 In what ways might **3.3** be seen as a statement of the religious and civil establishment?

In spite of the hostile attitude of **3.3** to reform, James demonstrated his ecclesiastical supremacy by presiding over the Hampton Court Conference.

3.4 William Barlow[1] on The Hampton Court Conference, 1604

First Day (14 January 1604)

[The king began] with a most grave and princely declaration of his general drift in calling this assembly, no novel device, but according to the example of all Christian princes, who in the commencement of their reign usually take the first course for the establishing of the Church, both for doctrine and policy ... [He assured] us that he called not this assembly for any innovation, acknowledging the government   5
ecclesiastical as now it is to have been approved by manifold blessings from God himself ... and in that he had received many complaints since his first entrance into the kingdom, especially through the dissensions in the Church, of many disorders as he heard, and much disobedience to the laws, with a great falling away to Popery; his purpose therefore was, like a good physician, to examine and try the complaints ...   10

Second Day (16 January 1604)

... Dr Reynolds ... reduced all matters disliked or questioned into these four heads:

1 That the doctrine of the Church might be preserved in purity, according to God's Word.
2 That good pastors might be planted in all churches to preach the same.
3 That the Church government might be seriously ministered, according to God's   15 Word.
4 That the Book of Common Prayer might be fitted to more increase of piety ...

[Dr Reynolds] moved his Majesty that there might be a new translation of the Bible ...

... Whereupon his Highness wished, that some especial pains should be taken in that behalf for one uniform translation ...   20

... [Concerning] the Planting of Ministers learned in every parish; it pleased his Majesty to answer ... [that] this matter was not for a present resolution, because to appoint to every parish a sufficient minister were impossible, the Universities would not afford them; Again, he had found already that he had more learned men in this

Realm than he had sufficient maintenance for … 25

Dr Reynolds … desired that … they of the Clergy might have meetings once every three weeks; first in Rural Deaneries, and therein to have Prophesying [meetings to discuss the Scriptures] … and that things, as could not be resolved upon there might be referred to the Archdeacon's Visitation; and so from thence to the Episcopal Synod, where the Bishop with his Presbyteri should determine all such points as before could not be decided. 30

At which speech his Majesty was somewhat stirred … thinking, that they aimed at a Scottish Presbytery, 'which', said he, 'as well agreeth with a Monarchy, as God and the Devil. Then Jack & Tom, & Will & Dick, shall meet, and at their pleasure censure me and my Council and all our proceedings …' 35

And then putting his hand to his hat, his Majesty said, 'My Lords the Bishops. I may thank you, that these men [Dr Reynolds etc] do thus plead for my Supremacy … But if once you were out, and they in place, I know what would become of my Supremacy. No Bishop, no King, as before I said …' and rising from his chair, as he was going to his inner Chamber, 'If this be all', quoth he, 'that they have to say, I shall make them conform themselves, or I will harry them out of the land, or else do worse.' 40

Third Day (18 January 1604)

… [His] Majesty shut up all with a most pithy exhortation to both sides for unity … To which they all gave their unanimous assent … Finally, they jointly promised to be quiet and obedient, now they knew it to be the King's mind to have it so …

[1] Barlow was Dean of Chester at the time of the conference, and subsequently Bishop of Rochester.

William Barlow, *Sum and Substance of the Conference*, quoted in R. Ashton, *James I by His Contemporaries*, 1969, pp. 176–86

3.5 An anonymous account of the Hampton Court Conference

His Majesty utterly distasting [Reynolds' scheme] said that this was rightly the presbytery of Scotland, wherein John and William and Richard and such like must have their censure, and John will give his vote, as William does for he is a godly man, and so all the matter is ordered by simple ignorant men. Whereto said Mr Knewstubbs if it please your Majesty he means a presbytery only of ministers and not of lay men. To whom said his Majesty I ken [understand] him well enough. And when I mean to live under a presbytery, I will go into Scotland again. But while I am in England, I will have bishops for I had not been so quietly settled in my seat but for them, adding that he had sufficiently tasted of the mischiefs thereof of a presbytery in Scotland … 5

F. Shriver, 'Hampton Court Revisited: James I and the Puritans', *Journal of Ecclesiastical History*, vol. 33, 1982

Questions

1   In the light of **3.1, 3.4, 3.5** and your own knowledge, what were the
    motives of James I for calling the Hampton Court Conference?

2   What evidence is there in **3.4** and **3.5** to suggest that the most important
    consideration for James was that of royal supremacy over the Church?

3   It is generally accepted that James conceded very little to Reynolds and
    the reformers at Hampton Court. Apart from the Authorized Version of
    the Bible the bishops dragged their heels in implementing the very few
    small liturgical changes. What explanations might be offered for this and
    which do you consider to be the most convincing? Use **3.6** and **3.7** in
    conjunction with earlier extracts and your own knowledge.

3.6, 3.7 and **3.8** all show an urgent desire for conformity after Hampton Court.
The message is urged in the Commons, in a royal proclamation from the king
in Council, and by royal assent to the Canons of 1604 issued by the new
Archbishop of Canterbury, Richard Bancroft.

3.6 James I to the Commons, 22 March 1604

At my first coming, although I found but one religion, and that which by myself is
professed, publicly allowed, and by the Law maintained; yet found I another sort of
religion besides, a private sect, lurking within the bowels of this nation. The first is
the true religion, which by me is professed, and by the Law is established: the second
is the falsely called Catholics, but truly Papists: the third (which I would call a Sect,   5
rather than a religion) is the Puritans and Novelists, who do not so far differ from us
in points of religion, as in their confused form of policy and parity; being ever so
discontented with the present government, and impatient to suffer any superiority;
which maketh their sect unable to be suffered in any well governed Commonwealth
… I acknowledge the Roman Church to be our mother church, although defiled with   10
some infirmities and corruptions … Let [the Papists] assure themselves, that, as I am
a friend to their persons, if they be good subjects, so am I a vowed enemy, and do
denounce mortal war to their errors.

The Journal of the House of Commons, vol. 1, p. 144

3.7 A proclamation enjoining conformity to the established form of the service of God, 16 July 1604

[We] have thought good once again to give notice thereof to all our subjects by public
declaration … there appeareth no cause why the form of the Service of God wherein
they have been nourished so many years should be changed; and consequently to
admonish them all in general to conform themselves thereunto, without listening to
the troublesome spirits of some persons who never receive contentment, either in   5

civil or ecclesiastical matters, but in their own fantasies, especially of certain
ministers who, under pretended zeal of reformation, are the chief authors of
divisions and sects among our people ... And yet ... we have thought good to give
time to all ministers disobedient to the orders of the Church and to ecclesiastical
authority here by law established, and who for such disobedience ... have incurred   10
any censures of the Church or penalties of laws, until the last of November now next
ensuing to bethink themselves of the course they will hold therein ... In which mean
time they may resolve either to conform themselves to the Church of England and
obey the same, or else to dispose of themselves and their families some other ways, as
to them shall seem meet ...

Stuart Royal Proclamations, vol. 1, *Royal Proclamations of King James I,
1603–25*, ed. J. F. Larkin and P. L. Hughes, 1973, no. 41, p. 87

3.8 The Canons of 1604

IV   Whosoever shall hereafter affirm, That the form of God's worship in the
Church of England established by law and contained in the Book of Common
Prayer ... is a corrupt, superstitious or unlawful worship of God, or containeth
anything that is repugnant to the Scriptures, let him be excommunicated ipso
facto, and not restored but only by the archbishop, and after his repentance and   5
public revocation of those his wicked errors.

V   Whosoever shall hereafter affirm, That any of the nine and thirty Articles
agreed upon by the archbishops and bishops of both provinces and the whole
of the clergy in Convocation ... in 1562 ... are in any part superstitious or
erroneous, or such as he may not with a good conscience subscribe unto; let him   10
be excommunicated ...

VI   Whosoever shall hereafter affirm, That the rites and ceremonies of the Church
of England by law established are wicked, anti-Christian, or superstitious ... let
him be excommunicated ...

VII Whosoever shall hereafter affirm, That the government of the Church of   15
England under his Majesty by archbishops, bishops, deans, archdeacons and the
rest that bear office in the same, is anti-Christian or repugnant to the Word of
God; let him be excommunicated ...

XXXVI Subscription required of such as are to be made Ministers

I   That the King's Majesty, under God, is the only supreme governor of this
realm, and of all other his Highness's dominions and countries, as well in all   20
spiritual or ecclesiastical things or causes as temporal; and that no foreign prince,
person, prelate, state or potentate hath, or ought to have, any jurisdiction, power,
superiority, pre-eminence or authority, ecclesiastical or spiritual, within his
Majesty's said realms, dominions and countries.

II   That the Book of Common Prayer, and of ordering of bishops, priests and   25
deacons, containeth in it nothing contrary to the Word of God ... and that he
himself will use the form in the said Book prescribed in public prayer and
administration of the sacraments, and none other.

III [That] he acknowledgeth all and every the articles ... being in number nine and thirty, to be agreeable to the Word of God.

Kenyon, *The Stuart Constitution*, p. 137

3.9 Nicolo Molin, Venetian ambassador in England, to the doge and Senate, 30 March 1605

Articles have been drawn up, and the Puritan ministers are called upon to sign them or to lose their benefices. There are many gentlemen who administer justice in their various counties and towns, and it is intended to make them sign these articles, and to promise to put down the Puritans within their various jurisdictions; if they refuse they will be removed from the Commission of the Peace. Many ministers and many   5
justices refused to subscribe, in the hope that the King would mitigate his orders, but seeing that he stands firm they have finally yielded and obeyed. On the other hand the persecution of the Catholics is vigorously conducted, all suspect houses are searched, and if crosses or anything indicating the Catholic religion is found the owner is imprisoned.

Cal State Papers Venetian, vol. 10, p. 232

3.10 A dialogue between Irenaeus and Antimachus, dedicated to Archbishop Bancroft, about the rites and ceremonies of the Church of England

ANTIMACHUS I am sad indeed, because ... for conscience sake only, I am deprived of my living.

IRENAEUS ... I marvel it should be so in this Realm of England, where the gospel is freely preached by public authority, and the preachers thereof are so countenanced by the king and state. I fear you are not conformable to   5
the discipline of the Church; and so have offended the law in that case, for which you are so censured.

[They agree to debate the issues]

ANTIMACHUS I differ chiefly from you in two points: namely in the garments of the ministers, and especially in the surplice; but most of all in the cross in baptism ... The people, to feed their fancies, do more regard such   10
apparel, than the preaching of him that weareth it.

IRENAEUS It would not be so if the outward ornaments of the Church be but such, as commonly have been used, especially if they be plain as the surplice ... and the habit of our ministers and bishops is. For the use, and the plainness of them prevent and take away all manner of   15
admiration ...

ANTIMACHUS You have said in the matter of garments enough, and I hold them to be tolerable. But that which stabbeth my conscience, is the cross in baptism. And this is the hook I cannot swallow: (i) because it is a

dangerous addition to the institution of the sacrament: (ii) there is no   20
warrant in the word of God for it: (iii) and no one thing so much as
that, hath been superstitiously abused: (iv) and there is no use of it.

Samuel Gardiner DD, 1605 (British Library Tract)

Questions

1   Using your own knowledge and information from **3.7–3.10**, discuss in
     what ways and with what success James I had followed a policy of
     religious conformity in England up to 1605?
2   What do you consider to be the significance of James's statement, 'I
     acknowledge the Roman Church to be our mother church …' [**3.6, line
     10; 3.12**]?
3   Discuss the view that Bancroft's Canons [**3.8, 3.10, 3.26**] strengthened
     rather than weakened the Church of England.
4   How far would you agree that the debate in **3.10** represents differences in
     externals rather than matters of substance in the Church of England?

The Roman Catholic problem: early attitude of James

3.11 A letter to Sir Robert Cecil, December? 1602

… I greatly wonder … that not only so great flocks of Jesuits and priests dare both
resort and remain in England but so proudly do use their functions through all the
parts of England without any controlment or punishment these divers years past … I
know it may be justly thought that I have the like beam in my own eye but, alas, it is a
far more barbarous and stiff-necked people that I rule over. Saint George surely rides   5
upon a towardly riding horse where I am daily burstin in daunting a wild unruly colt.
And I protest, in God's presence, the daily increase I hear of popery in England, and
the proud vanterie[1] that the papists make daily there of their power, their increase,
and their combined faction that none shall enter to be king there but by their
permission.

[1] vanterie = boasting

The Letters of King James VI and I, ed. G. P. V. Akrigg, 1984, no. 89

3.12 A letter to Sir Robert Cecil, March? 1603

My dearest 10 [a cipher for Sir Robert Cecil]

… I did ever hate alike both extremities in any case, only allowing the middes[1] for
virtue, as by my book now lately published[2] doth plainly appear … I will never allow
in my conscience that the blood of any man shall be shed for diversity of opinions in

religion, but I would be sorry that Catholics should so multiply as they might be able 5
to practise their old principles upon us ... I long to see the execution of the last edict
against them, not that thereby I wish to have their heads divided from their bodies
but that I would be glad to have both their heads and bodies separated from this
whole island and safely transported beyond the seas ...

No! I am so far from any intention of persecution as, I protest to God, I reverence 10
their church as our mother church although clogged with many infirmities and
corruptions, besides that I did ever hold persecution as one of the infallible notes of
a false church ...

Your most loving friend,
30 [James R]

[1] middes = the middle way
[2] *The Basilikon Doron*

Akrigg, *Letters*, **no. 91**

3.13 A letter to Henry Percy, Earl of Northumberland, 24 March 1603

... As for the Catholics, I will neither persecute any that will be quiet and give but an
outward obedience to the law, neither will I spare to advance any of them that will by
good service worthily deserve it ...

Akrigg, *Letters*, **no. 92**

Questions

1   In what ways does James suggest that his religious problems in Scotland
    were greater than those he might have had in England?
2   What evidence is there in **3.11**, **3.12** and **3.13** that James was
    discriminating in his attitude to Roman Catholics?
3   Why might English Roman Catholics expect a better deal from James
    than they had had from Elizabeth?

The Gunpowder Plot, 1605

3.14 A Letter from the Earl of Salisbury to Sir Charles Cornwallis, 9 November 1605

It hath pleased Almighty God out of his singular Goodness, to bring to light the
most cruel and detestable Conspiracy against the person of his Majesty and the
whole State of this realme that ever was conceived by the Hart of Man ... The
meanes how to have compassed so great an Acte, was not to be performed by
Strength of men, or outward Violence, but by a secret Conveyence of a great 5

Quantitie of Gunpowder in a Vault under the Upper House of parliament, and so to have blowne up all at a Clapp, if God out of his Mercie and just Revenge against so great an Abomination had not destined it to be discovered, though very miraculously even some twelve Houres before the Matter should have been put into Execution. The Person that was the principal Undertaker of it, is one Johnson, a Yorkshire man   10 and Servant to one Thomas Percy, a Gentleman Pensioner to his Majestie, and a near Kinsman to the Earl of Northumberland.

This Percy had about a Year and a half agoe hyred a Part of Viniard House in the Old Palace, from whence he had access into this Vault to lay his Wood and Cole … Johnson had at sundry Times very privately conveyed a great Quantity of Powder,   15 and therewith filled two Hogsheads, and some thirty two small Barrels; all which he had cunningly covered with a great store of Billets and Faggots; and on Monday at Night, as he was busie to prepare his things for Execution, was apprehended in the Place itself, with a false Lanthorne, booted and spurred …

It remaineth that I add something … how this Matter came to be discovered. About   20 eight Days before the parliament should have begunn, the Lord Mounteagle received a Letter about six a Clock at Night, (which was delivered to his Footman in the Dark to give him) without Name or Date, and in a Hand disguised … As soon as he imparted the same unto mee … I could not well distinguish whether it were Frenzy or Sport … Nevertheless, being loath to trust my own Judgment alone … I imparted   25 the Letter to the Earl of Suffolk, Lord Chamberlain … whereupon perusing the Words of the Letter … we both conceaved, that it could not be more proper than the time of parliament, nor by any other way like to be attempted than with Powder, whilst the King was sitting in that Assembly; of which the Lord Chamberlain conceaved more probability, because there was a great Vault under the said Chamber,   30 which was never used for any thing but for some Wood and Cole … [After] we had imparted the same to the Lord Admirall, the Earl of Worcester, the Earl of Northampton, and some others, we all thought fitt to forbeare to impart it to the King untill some three or four Daies before the Sessions. At which time we shewed his majestie the Letter …   35

Whereupon his Majestie, who hath a naturall Habit to contemne all false Fears, and a Judgment so strong as never to doubt any thing which is not well warranted by reason, concurred thus farr with us, that seeing such a matter was possible, that should be done which might prevent all danger or nothing at all …

Since the Writing of this Letter we have assured News that those Traytors are   40 overthrowne by the Sherriff of Worcestershire, after they had betaken themselves for their Safetie in a Retreate to the house of Stephen Littleton in Staffordshire. The House was fired by the Sheriff; at the issuing forth Catesby was slaine, Percy sore hurt, Graunte and Wrighte burned in their Faces with Gun-powder; the rest are either taken or slaine.

R. Ashton, *James I by His Contemporaries*, 1969, pp. 192–96

3.15 Nicolo Molin, Venetian ambassador in England, to the doge and Senate, 16 November 1605

About six months ago ... Thomas Percy, relation of the Earl of Northumberland, and pensioner of the King, hired ... some wine cellars under the place where parliament meets, and stored in them some barrels of beer ... wood and coal. He said he meant to open a tavern for the use of servants who attended their masters to parliament. But among this beer, wood, and coals he introduced thirty-three barrels   5
of gunpowder, besides four tuns ... intending to make use of it at the right moment. About two months ago Lord Salisbury received anonymous letters from France, warning him to be on his guard, for a great conspiracy was being hatched by priests and Jesuits; but, as similar information had been sent about a year ago ... no great attention was paid to these letters ... Finally, on Monday last, a letter was brought by   10
an unknown person, for it was dark, about two o'clock of the night, to a servant of Lord Monteagle, who was standing at the door. The unknown said, 'Please give this to your master; and tell him to reply at once, as I will come back in half an hour for the answer to carry to my master.' The [servant] ... gave it to his master, who opened it and found it was anonymous, nor did he recognise the hand. The substance of the   15
letter was this, that the writer, in return for the favours received at various times from Lord Monteagle, had resolved to warn him by letter that he should on no account attend parliament the following morning, as he valued his life, for the good party in England had resolved to execute the will of God, which was to punish the King ... and the Ministers for their bitter persecution against the poor [Catholics]   20
... Lord Monteagle read the letter, and in great astonishment took it to the Earl of Salisbury, who at once carried it to the King ... The King read the letter, and in terrified amaze he said, 'I remember that my father died by gunpowder ... I see the letter says the blow is to be struck on a sudden. Search the basements of the meeting place.' The Chamberlain, with three or four attendants, went straightway to carry   25
out this order ... After shifting the wood he found underneath some barrels of powder, and after shifting the coal he found more barrels. In confusion he returned to the King and told him; and orders were at once given ... to set sentinels in various posts to watch who approached the doors of the cellars. About two in the morning they saw a man approaching with a dark lantern ... The guards cunningly drew back   30
and left him free passage to the cellars ... The man went in, laid a train of powder and fitted a slow match ... His intention was to fire the train in the morning. When he had finished his business, as he was coming out, he was surprised by the guard, who asked what [he was doing] at that hour at that place. [He replied] that he had come there, as he had a fancy to see his property. They saw a bag in his hand, and   35
found in it little bits of a slow match, and when they turned on the light they saw the train of powder. Thereupon they bound him and took him to the Palace, where some of the Council were awake, waiting the issue of this affair ...

Cal State Papers Venetian, vol. 10, p. 288

3.16 Nicolo Molin, Venetian ambassador in England, to the doge and Senate, 21 November 1605

The King had let it be known that he wished to have the Scots about his person, as he has not much confidence in the English, who know this and are greatly annoyed. The King is in terror; he does not appear nor does he take his meals in public as usual. He lives in the innermost rooms, with only Scotchmen about him. The Lords of the Council are also alarmed and confused by the plot itself and the King's   5
suspicions; the city is in great uncertainty; Catholics fear heretics and vice-versa; both are armed; foreigners live in terror of their houses being sacked by the mob that is convinced that some, if not all, foreign Princes are at the bottom of the plot.

Cal State Papers Venetian, vol. 10, p. 293

3.17 Sir Edward Hoby to Sir Thomas Edmondes, 19 November 1605

On the 5th of November we began our parliament, when the king should have come in person, but he refrained through a practice but that morning discovered. The plot was to have blown up the king at such time as he should have been set in his royal throne, accompanied with his children, nobility, and commoners, and assisted with all bishops, judges, and doctors, at one instant; a blast to have ruined the whole state   5
and kingdom of England ...

When Johnson was brought to the king's presence, the king asked him how he could conspire so hideous treason against his children and so many innocent souls, which never offended him? He answered, that it was true; but a dangerous disease required a desperate remedy. He told some of the Scots that his intent was to have blown them   10
back again into Scotland.

T. Birch, *The Court and Times of James I*, vol. I, 1849, p. 36

3.18 The Gunpowder Plot

... Upon the discovery Percy, Catesby, Robert and Thomas Winter, fled from London into Warwickshire; where they raised the county ... From thence went into Staffordshire, being in all sixty or eighty horse; where, being pursued by the sheriff of Warwickshire, and seeing that the country stuck not to them as they thought, they took one Littleton's house [Holbeach House], which being by the sheriff aforesaid   5
beset, after some small resistance, were all taken, Percy and Catesbie being then slain, the rest brought up to London and committed to prison. Afterwards, upon examination of these captives, were apprehended the Earl of Northumberland, Lord Vaux, Lord Stourton, Lord Lumley, and the Lord Mordaunt, and committed to the tower.

The Diary of Walter Yonge esq. written at Colyton and Axminster, Co. Devon from 1604–1628, Camden Society, 1847, p. 2

Questions

1 In what ways does Salisbury's use of language and tone in **3.14** indicate his attitude to the plot?
2 How satisfactory is Salisbury's explanation of the delay in revealing the plot?
3 How convinced are you by Salisbury's description of the attitude of James I?
4 Does the Venetian ambassador's account of the discovery of the plot in **3.15** differ significantly from that of Salisbury in **3.14**?
5 What is the significance of the ambassador's phrase 'the good party in England' [**3.15, line 18**]?
6 Can the differing portraits of the king presented by the same ambassador in **3.15** and **3.16** be reconciled?
7 What indications are there in **3.14–3.18** that the plot was easily crushed both at the centre and in the localities?
8 What evidence is there in **3.16** and **3.17** that the plot has a 'British' dimension?

The aftermath of the plot

3.19 Sir Edward Hoby to Sir Thomas Edmondes, 10 February 1606

On the 21 January we began our parliament, and that day was passed in the House of Commons with motions tending that a committee might be chosen to consider certain points, which the speaker of the House should deliver unto the king, wishing that first there might be a congratulation from us all for his happy deliverance, and to move his majesty that he would make a public proclamation, in showing his detestation against Popery and their adherents; that his majesty would not use his wonted clemency against such offenders; and in the end to be petitioners unto his majesty on behalf of the House, that he would be pleased that we might make more severe laws against them than yet were ...

In Birch, *The Court and Times of James I*, vol. I, pp. 45ff.

3.20 The Earl of Salisbury to Sir Henry Wotton, 16 June 1606

Some acts have been made against the papists, which I cannot so properly term new laws, but rather explanations and directions for the better execution of former laws, which were in force against them, whereof they had always some shift or other to avoid the danger ... it was thought most necessary to provide for the execution of them, the additions being only in some cases, as an oath of allegiance to all, that will serve abroad, the contents whereof I sent you, which, in truth, is less than the supremacy.

Birch, *The Court and Times of James I*, vol. I, p. 64

3.21 The Oath of Allegiance, 1606

I A.B. do truly and sincerely acknowledge, profess, testify and declare in my
conscience before God and the world, That our sovereign lord King James is lawful
and rightful King of the realm, and of all other his Majesy's dominions and
countries; and that the pope neither of himself nor by any authority of the church
or of Rome, or by any other means with any other, hath any power or authority to   5
depose the King, or to dispose any of his majesty's kingdoms or dominions, or to
authorize any foreign prince to invade or annoy him or his countries, or to discharge
any of his subjects of their allegiance and obedience to his Majesty, or to give licence
or leave to any of them to bear arms, raise tumults or to offer any violence or hurt to
his Majesty's royal person, state or government, or to any of his Majesty's subjects   10
within his Majesty's dominions. Also I do swear from my heart, That notwithstanding any declaration or sentence of excommunication, or deprivation made or
granted, by the pope or his successors, or by any authority derived or pretended to
be derived from him or his see against the said King, his heirs or successors, or any
absolution of the said subjects from their obedience: I will bear faith and true   15
allegiance to his Majesty, his heirs and successors, and him and them will defend to
the uttermost of my power, against all conspiracies and attempts whatsoever which
shall be made against his or their persons, their crown and dignity, by reason or
colour of any such sentence or declaraton, or otherwise, and will do my best
endeavour to disclose and make known unto his majesty, his heirs and successors, all   20
treasons and traitorous conspiracies which I shall know or hear of to be against him
or any of them. And I do further swear, That I do from my heart abhor, detest and
abjure, as impious and heretical, this damnable doctrine and position. That princes
which be excommunicated or deprived by the Pope, may be deposed or murdered
by the subjects, or any other whatsoever. And I do believe, and in my conscience am   25
resolved, That neither the Pope nor any other person whatsoever, hath power to
absolve me of this oath or any part thereof, which I acknowledge by good and full
authority to be lawfully ministered unto me, and do renounce all pardons and
dispensations to the contrary. And all these things I do plainly and sincerely
acknowledge and swear, according to the express words by me spoken, and according   30
to the plain and common sense and understanding of the same words, without any
equivocation or mental evasion, or secret reservation whatsoever: and I do make this
recognition and acknowledgement heartily, willingly and truly, upon the true faith
of a christian.

So help me God.

James VI and I, *Collected Works*, 1616, pp. 250–52

3.22 A letter from Pope Paul V to English Catholics after the Oath of Allegiance

The tribulations and calamities, which you have continually sustained for the keeping
of the Catholic Faith, have always afflicted us with great grief of mind … [We] have
heard how you are compelled, by most grievous punishments set before you, to go to

the Churches of heretics … Yet notwithstanding … we are enforced to admonish and
desire you, that by no means you come within the Churches of Heretics, or hear their   5
Sermons, or communicate with them in their rites, lest you incur the wrath of God:
For these things may ye not do without damaging the worship of God, and your own
salvation. As likewise you cannot without most evident and grievous wronging of
God's Honour, bind yourselves by the Oath, which in like manner we have heard
with very great grief of our heart is administered unto you …

James VI and I, *Collected Works*, 1616, p. 250

3.23 Memorandum of the confiscated property of recusants, 25 September 1606

An Indenture of the goodes of John Dike of Kellinge, William Reeve of Wickmore,
and Thomas Seppins of Westrudham, Recusants found by the oath of Christopher
Parr … [23 other names follow]

John Dike, possessed of one shodd carte, One milch cowe, Two worke horses, Three
combes of Ryes, Three combes of Barley, One Table, Forretene peces of pewter,   5
Seaven peces of Brasse, Three speetes, One firepan and tonges, One bedsteede and a
stockbedd. One coverlet. Three chestes and two paire of sheetes. Et valent in tot. £8.

William Reve possessed of Tenn combes of wheate, Tenn combes of Rye, Twenty
combes of barley and five combes of Bucke, One olde geldinge, Two mares, Five
milch neate and two yearlinge calves. Et valent in tot. £16.   10

Thomas Seppins, possessed of Twenty combes of wheat, Twenty combes of Rye,
Forty combes of Barley, Three worke horses, Five milch neate and divers
implementes of household. Et valent in tot. £36.

*The Official Papers of Sir Nathaniel Bacon of Stiffkey, Norfolk, as Justice of
the Peace, 1580–1620*, **Camden Society, 3rd Series, vol. 26, 1915, p. 183**

Questions

1   Using the material in **3.19–3.23**, explain the measures taken against
    English Roman Catholics in the aftermath of the Gunpowder Plot.
2   Salisbury suggests in **3.20** a tightening of existing measures rather than
    new anti-Catholic legislation. Why had statutory measures against
    Roman Catholics such as seen in **3.23** not always been implemented?

The religious situation 1607–10

By 1607 uniformity of religion in England, let alone in Britain, had proved
elusive. Although the Venetian ambassador [**3.24**] had a problem in defining
Puritans as something other than Protestant, his summary of the king's religion is astute. Some interesting, if unverifiable, statistics emerge from **3.25**,

and **3.26** is a good example of a petition asking for the reinstatement of those who lost their benefices as a result of Bancroft's Canons. This is enlivened by the addition of James's marginal notes written in Scottish.

3.24 Report on England presented by Nicolo Molin, Venetian ambassador, to his Government, 1607

He [James I] is a Protestant, as it is called; that means a mixture of a number of religions; in doctrine he is Calvinistic, but not so in politics and policy; for Calvin denies authority not merely spiritual but temporal as well, a doctrine that will always be abhorred by every sovereign.

The nation embraces three religions, the Roman Catholic and Apostolic, the   5
Protestant and the Puritan. This latter, besides the ruin of souls, tends also to the
ruin of principalities and monarchs, for it is entirely directed to liberty and popular
government. Now, as the word liberty sounds sweet to everyone and is readily
embraced, we may believe that a third of the population is Puritan, although the
King and his Ministers employ every art to destroy them, and ... the sect instead   10
of declining is on the increase. The Protestant religion which is the King's, is
Calvinistic in doctrine, but very different in theory of government. It admits bishops
and high ecclesiastics, and of course the secular and royal authority. This religion
embraces another third of the population it is thought. The King tried to extend this
creed. His great desire is to have one religion ... The King is a bitter enemy of our   15
religion, not merely because he holds it to be full of abuses and corruption, but
because of this said impious and unjust doctrine [that subjects of a heretic Sovereign
are freed from oath of allegiance, and may with a clear conscience embark on
rebellion, sedition and conspiracy].

Cal State Papers Venetian, vol. 10, p. 511

3.25 A petition against scandalous ministers; non residency, plurality

... We are enforced, once again, to be most humble Petitioners unto your most
excellent Majesty, touching the late deprived, suspended, and silenced Ministers,
that they may be restored to the use of their Ministry ...

In the Dispute touching the Petition, it was, by occasion, delivered, that in England
there were,   5
8000 parish churches
Not 2000 resident preaching ministers
Not 1000 that preach once a month
Not 500 single-beneficed
300 deprived, suspended, or silenced   10
400 Jesuits and Seminaries [seminary priests] in England
40 simple people converted in a year by one Jesuit
300 convicted Recusants in a shire, at the Queen's death; now 800

The Journal of the House of Commons, vol. 1, p. 380

3.26 A request for toleration

The considerations … may induce your Majesty to yield us satisfaction … First, in that the Church government solicited by us, is more compatible with your Imperial sceptre and more advantageable thereto, than that of the said Prelates. Secondly, in that it standeth with the policy and reason of State to allow the toleration and exemption desired by us. Thirdly, in that the courses held by the said Prelates against 5 us, are for the extreme rigour and partiality of them such as your majesty upon due information received, cannot but in justice and commiseration afford us relief and redress.

[The point was made that the prelates' authority was conveyed by the Church of Rome]

Wherein as the said Prelates do cast an apparent blemish and dishonour upon the Gospel professed by your Majesty and your people, as if from and by the means of   10 Antichrist, the churches of Christ should receive the assurance and warrant of their ministry.

King James's note: A notorious and shameful lye.

[On the subject of parish pastors]

King James's note: millions of brainsick popes are more dangerous than one.

There is within your kingdom a faction of Romanists … Now this faction can not but 15 grow so much the more reinforced and potent, by how much the Protestant party shall be enfeebled and lessened. And the Protestant party can not but diminish and languish, in case the aforesaid course of the Prelates be continued.

King James's note [in good ripe Scottish!]: The Protestant partie cannot but languish indeed quhen as her bowellis are so gnawin by her owin viperouse and ungratiouse   20 broode, so as having a strong forraine adversary on the one syde, she is on the other partie never at reste within her owin doores … The too great toleration of you in queene Elizabeth's tyme hath made you now to be prikkels in oure sydes … Thaire can be no unitie in the Church if thair be no ordours nor obedience to superiors, but that it be lawful to everyman to follow freely his own fancie.

A Supplication for Toleration Addressed to King James I by Some of the Late Silenced and Deprived Ministers and People Consenting in Judgement with them, **1609, reprinted (with the king's hitherto unpublished notes) by the Rev. S. R. Maitland, London, 1859**

Questions

1   In the light of the evidence from **3.24** and **3.25**, how might you argue that the Church of England was in a worse state by 1607 than it had been in 1603?

2   How reliable is the evidence of the authors of **3.24** and **3.25**?

3   Who were the silenced and deprived ministers [3.26]? How strong are the arguments for their restoration advanced?
4   'Millions of brainsick popes are more dangerous than one' [**3.26, line 14**]. Explain this statement and discuss the validity of the assertion.

The Book of Sports

3.27 The king's declaration to his subjects concerning lawful sports, 1618

It is true that at our first entry to this Crown and Kingdom we were informed, and that too truly, that our County of Lancashire abounded more in Popish recusants than any county of England ...

The report of this growing amendment amongst them made us the more sorry when with our own ears we heard the general complaint of our people that they were   5
barred from all lawful recreation and exercise upon the Sunday's afternoon after the ending of all Divine Service, which cannot but produce two evils: the one, the hindering of the conversion of many whom their priests will take occasion hereby to vex, persuading them that no honest mirth or recreation is lawful or tolerable in our religion, which cannot but breed a great discontentment in our people's hearts,   10
especially of such as are peradventure upon the point of turning; the other inconvenience is, that this prohibition barreth the common and meaner sort of people from using such exercises as may make their bodies more able for war, when we or our successors shall have occasion to use them, and in place thereof sets up filthy tipplings and drunkenness, and breeds a number of idle and discontented   15
speeches in their ale-houses. For when shall the common people have leave to exercise if not upon the Sundays and Holy Days, seeing they must apply their labour and win their living in all working days?

... And as for our good people's lawful recreation, our pleasure likewise is, that after the end of Divine Service our good people be not disturbed ... from any lawful   20
recreation; such as dancing, either men or women, archery for men, leaping, vaulting, or any other such harmless recreation, nor from having of May-games, Whitsun ales, and morris-dances, and the setting up of May-poles and other sports therewith used, so as the same be had in due and convenient time, without impediment or neglect of Divine Service ...

J. R. Tanner, *Constitutional Documents of the Reign of James I, 1603–1625*, 1961, pp. 54–56

3.28 A sabbatarian challenge

Item, it is informed that uppon the first day of August last 1619 William Clough, Clerke, did preach within the parish Church of Bramham ... upon the text Thou shalt keepe my Sabboath. And in his preaching did utter these woordes following ... Nowe in deed the king of Heaven doth bid you keepe his Sabboath and reverens his

sanctuarie. Nowe the king of England is a mortal man and he bids you breake it.   5
Chuse whether of them you will followe.

The articles of informacion exhibited by Edmond Troutbecke against William Clough, Clerke, together with the disposicion of the witnesses thereupon in breefe manner, 7 **March 1620**, in *Calendar of State Papers Domestic, James I*, vol. **113**, p. 13

Questions

1   What advantages did James hope to gain from the Declaration on Sports?
2   Would you regard it as anti-Catholic or anti-Puritan in intention?
3   How far does **3.28** explain Puritan hostility to the declaration?

Problems in Britain and Europe – the end of the reign

The outbreak of the Thirty Years War sharpened both religious divisions and definitions [**3.29, 3.30**]. It also raised the spectre of the power of the pulpit as 'rash heady' preachers began 'to meddle with matters of State'. Before the collapse of the Spanish marriage brought about the rehabilitation of James's religious orthodoxy, censorship in the form of the 1622 Directions to Preachers [**3.31**] was necessary.

3.29 A view of the changing meanings of Puritanism, Protestantism and Catholicism, early 1620s

Time was, a PURITAN was counted such
As held some Ceremonies were too much ...

Time was, a PROTESTANT was only taken
For such as had the Church of Rome forsaken ...

Time was, a PAPIST was a man who thought   5
Rome could not err, but all her Canons ought
To be canonical; and, blindly led,
He from the Truth, for fear of Error, fled.

But now these words, with divers others more,
Have other senses than they had before ...   10

A Puritan
(So nicknamed, but indeed the sound Protestant.)

A Puritan is such another thing
As says, with all his heart, 'GOD save the King
And all his issue!' and to make this good,

Will freely spend his money and his blood;
And in his factious and fond mood, dare say,   15
'Tis madness, for the Palsgrave, thus to stay
And wait the loving leisure of kind Spain!
...
A Puritan is he, that speaks his mind
In Parliament ... He crosseth not
This man, because a Courtier or a Scot ...   20

A Protestant

A Protestant is such another thing
As makes, within his heart, God of the King ...

A Protestant is one that shakes his head
And pities much the Palsgrave[1] was misled
To meddle with Bohemia, and incense   25
The Spanish wrath; 'gainst which, there is no fence! ...

A Protestant, no other fault can spy
In all Rome's beadroll of iniquity,
But that, of late, they do profess King-killing;
Which Catholic point, to credit he's unwilling ...   30

A Protestant is he, whose good intention
Deserves an English and a Spanish pension ...

A Papist

A Romanist is such another thing
As would, with all his heart, murder the King ...

Let him to Church resort, or be Recusant;   35
All's one! he's counted a good Protestant.
Nay, 'tis a question, if GUY FAWKES were one!
But 'tis resolved that Papist, he was none.
His Character abridged, if you will have,
HE IS SPAIN'S SUBJECT, AND A ROMISH SLAVE!

[1] the Palsgrave = The Elector Palatine

The Interpreter, wherin three principal Terms of State, much mistaken by the vulgar are clearly unfolded in C. H. **Firth**, *Stuart Tracts, 1603–1693*, 1964, pp. 234ff.

3.30 Owen Felltham on Puritans, *c.* 1623

I find many that are called Puritans, yet few, or none that will own the name. Whereof the reason sure is this, that 'tis for the most part held a name of infamy; and is so new, that it hath scarcely yet obtained definition: nor is it an appelation derived from one man's name, whose tenets we may find digested into a volume: whereby we

do much err in the application. It imports a kind of excellency above another, which 5
man (being conscious of his own frail bendings) is ashamed to assume to himself. So
that I believe there are men that would be Puritans; but indeed not any that are. One
will have him one that lives religiously ... Another, him that separates from our
divine assemblies. Another, him that in some tenets only is peculiar. Another, him
that will not swear. Absolutely to define him is a work, I think, of difficulty. Some I 10
know that rejoice in the name, but sure they be such as least understand it. As he is
more generally in these times taken, I suppose we may call him a Church-rebel, or
one that would exclude order that his brain might rule ...

F. Scott, *The Stuart Age, Commentaries of an Era*, 1974, p. 178

3.31 The king's letter to the Archbishop of Canterbury giving directions to preachers, 4 August 1622

I   That no preacher under the degree and calling of a Bishop or Dean ... do take
occasion, by the expounding of any text of Scripture whatsoever, to fall into any
set discourse ... otherwise than by opening the coherence ... of the text, which
shall not be comprehended ... within some one of the Articles of Religion ...

II   That no parson [etc] shall preach any sermon ... upon Sundays and holy days in 5
the afternoon in any cathedral or parish church throughout the kingdom but
upon some part of the Catechism or some text taken out of the Creed, Ten
Commandments, or the Lord's Prayer (funeral sermons only excepted) ...

III   That no preacher of what title so ever under the degree of a Bishop, or a Dean at
the least, do from henceforth presume to preach in any popular auditory the 10
deep points of predestination, election, reprobation, or of the universality,
efficacy, resistibility or irresistibilty, of God's grace ...

IV   That no preacher of what title or denomination soever from henceforth shall
presume in any auditory within this kingdom to declare, or limit ... in any
lecture or sermon the power, prerogative, and jurisdiction, authority, or duty of 15
Sovereign Princes, or otherwise meddle with matters of State ...

V   That no preacher of what title or denomination soever shall ... fall into bitter
invectives and undecent railing speeches against the persons of either Papists or
Puritans ...

VI   Lastly, that the Archbishops and Bishops ... (whom his Majesty hath good cause 20
to blame for their former remissness) be more wary and choice in their licensing
of preachers ...

J. Rushworth, *Historical Collections*, 1659, vol. 1, p. 64

Questions

1   In what ways and to what extent did the terms Puritan, Protestant and
Papist change during the reign of James I according to the author of
3.29?

2   Why does the author of **3.30** differentiate between a Protestant and a Puritan?
3   Compare and contrast the definitions of a Puritan offered by **3.29** and **3.30**.
4   Why did James issue the directions to preachers in 1622? Do they represent a response to the invasion of royal prerogative rather than religious censorship?
5   To what extent did James secure a compromise in religion in Britain?

Recommended reading

R. J. Acheson, *Radical Puritans in England, 1550–1660*, 1990
S. Babbage, *Puritanism and Richard Bancroft*, 1982
P. Collinson, *The Religion of Protestants: The Church in English Society 1559–1625*, 1982
P. Collinson, 'The Jacobean religious settlement: the Hampton Court Conference' in H. Tomlinson (ed.), *Before the English Civil War*, 1983
M. H. Curtis, 'The Hampton Court Conference and its aftermath', *History*, vol. 46, 1961
R. Cust and A. Hughes (eds.), *Conflict in Early Stuart England*, 1989 (for articles by P. Lake on anti-popery and T. Cogswell on the Spanish marriage)
A. Dures, *English Catholicism 1558–1642*, 1983
K. Fincham, *Prelate as Pastor: The Episcopate of James I*, 1990
K. Fincham and P. Lake, 'The ecclesiastical policy of James I', *Journal of British Studies*, vol. 24, 1985
P. Lake, 'Calvinism and the English Church 1570–1635', *Past and Present*, no. 114, 1987
P. Lake, *Anglicans and Puritans? Presbyterians and the English Conformist Thought from Whitgift to Hooker*, 1988
A. J. R. Smith (ed.), *The Reign of James VI and I*, 1973 (for a useful article by J. Bossy on the English Catholic Community)
H. Trevor-Roper, *Catholics and Anglicans and Puritans*, 1990
M. Todd (ed.), *Reformation to Revolution: Politics and Religion in Early Modern England*, 1995 (for a collection of key articles from historical journals)
N. R. N. Tyacke, 'Puritanism, Arminianism and Counter Revolution' in C. Russell (ed.), *The Origins of the English Civil War*, 1973
N. R. N. Tyacke, *Anti-Calvinists: The Rise of English Arminianism*, 1987
J. Wormald, 'Gunpowder, treason, and Scots', *Journal of British Studies*, vol. 24, 1985
P. White, 'The rise of Arminianism reconsidered', *Past and Present*, no. 101, 1983

4 'The state of monarchy is the supremest thing upon earth.' James I and Parliament

The Third Parliament, 30 January 1621 to 6 January 1622

The Palatinate problem
Supplies for intervention
Impeachment
Spanish marriage
Privilege
The Commons Petition
The Protestation

The Fourth Parliament, 19 February 1624 to 27 March 1625
(prorogued 29 May 1624 and dissolved on the death of James in March 1625)

The question of war
Subsidies
Monopolies Act
Impeachment of Cranfield
Defensive alliance with the United Provinces
Negotiations with France
Marriage between Prince Charles and Henrietta Maria agreed
Mansfeld's expedition raised

Maurice Lee has calculated that during the twenty-two years of the reign of James I, the English Parliament was in session for about thirty-six months. Two conclusions may be drawn from this. The first is that the so-called Whig interpretation of a confrontational Jacobean Parliament winning the initiative from James I and striding out on the 'high road to Civil War' is hardly likely in only thirty-six months of encounter. Alternatively, relations between Crown and Parliament were indeed so contentious that James avoided them as much as possible, especially after the First Parliament. The most reasonable assumption is, however, that James used his Parliaments in exactly the same way as most contemporary sovereigns: for advice, legislation and subsidies.

The curse of historical hindsight has exercised a tremendous influence on the interpretation of events of the seventeenth century. Explanations of the origins of dramatic events such as the Civil War have distorted assessments of the parliamentary management of James I; the long-term unresolved problems of Crown–Parliament relations are so easily ascribed to a foreign, Scottish king unable to halt the dysfunctional trends at the end of Elizabeth's reign, thus allowing 'the winning of the initiative' by the House of Commons and the formation of a parliamentary 'Opposition' with a capital 'O' (in the words of Wallace Notestein's 1924 British Academy Lecture). It was not until

1976 with the publication of Conrad Russell's article 'Parliamentary history in perspective, 1604–29' in *History* that the focus was placed on the demands of war in the 1620s as the catalyst in speeding up the disintegration of an already dysfunctional structure, rather than on blunders by James I. This is not to say that there was no opposition with a small 'o' voiced in Jacobean Parliaments nor that the ability of the Commons to slip the Speaker's control by use of the committee system and committee of the whole House was not employed.

As part of the business of Parliament was to hear grievances, it was inevitable that contentious issues would be raised. There was no shortage of these. In the First Parliament (1604–11), issues of feudal fiscal devices such as wardship and purveyance were raised [5.12, 5.13], as were matters of parliamentary privileges over electoral procedures in Shirley's case [4.5] and the Buckinghamshire election dispute [4.6]. The Form of Apology and Satisfaction [4.7], although never presented to the king, is a powerful document in its assertions of privilege. Obstruction of the king's scheme for union and style, opposition to impositions [4.10], the reaction to Dr Cowell's *Interpreter* [4.8] and the failure of the Great Contract [5.21–5.23] show the difficulties James faced in the First Parliament. 'The Addled Parliament' of 1614 highlights James's failure to pack Parliament [4.13, 4.14]; its attempts to debate impositions produced an early dissolution as the king's ultimate weapon in controlling faction.

Deteriorating royal finances and the demands for support of the cause of the Palatinate abroad produced heated exchanges in the Third Parliament (1621) over patents and monopolies [5.28], which was also marked by the fall of Bacon as a victim to the renewed use of the device of impeachment. Its highlight was a series of exchanges on foreign policy between James and the Commons that were rooted in the misty parameters of royal prerogative and parliamentary privilege [4.23–4.27]. In the 1624 Parliament, as the unholy, albeit temporary, alliance of Prince Charles, Buckingham (James's favourite) and the Commons sought to steer the unwilling king towards the abandonment of his foreign policy, James made concessions in the form of a Monopolies Act, an agreement to discuss foreign policy, and the establishment of a committee on the supply of funds for war.

The issues chronicled above were real. What is open to debate is how serious they were. It must be remembered that parliamentary sessions were short and that no organised opposition emerged deliberately seeking to undermine the capacity of James to rule. The cut and thrust of politics frequently had its origins in vested interest organised at best into somewhat fluid factions; the initiative in dominating faction whether at court, Council or in Parliament was regularly seized by James – faction-bashing was a life skill learnt in Scotland. James had, moreover, a genuine and sincere desire to avoid deep contention. When this threatened he would either compromise (as in the Buckinghamshire elections), yield (as in the case of Dr Cowell's book [4.8]), or use his prerogative to prorogue or dissolve Parliament.

That King James was aware of his unique position can be seen in his writings [4.1, 4.2] before his accession to the English throne, and in his speeches to the Westminster Parliament [4.3, 4.4]. The elaborate and mystical theory of the Divine Right of Kings may suggest a degree of insecurity in his claim to the English throne; none, however, could deny the Divine Will. The theory of the Divine Right of Kings asserted that a king ruled by virtue of the fact that God had chosen him for that office, making him God's lieutenant on earth. It followed that the king was responsible to God alone for his actions and to disobey the king was to sin. It stressed the sanctity of monarchy as the traditional, divinely ordained authority. It buttressed James as supreme governor of the Church, fountain and interpreter of law, and the wielder of emergency power. It was a doctrine particularly suited to a king who wished to safeguard his position as head of the Church as well as of the State. It finds supreme artistic expression in the *Apotheosis of James I*, the central panel in the Banqueting House ceiling. As long as it never became an absolute monarchy, it was in the interests of both Houses either to pay lip service to the idea of Divine Right or to ignore it. By virtue of its appeal to the divinely ordained social hierarchy and its implicit guarantee of peace, harmony and stability, it safeguarded the balance of an essentially elitist society. In any case, James was very keen to show the differences between a 'just king' and 'a usurping tyrant'. The key difference was the respect for law which characterised the former. James I was well aware that he had not merely rights but obligations to his subjects.

The royal prerogative inherited with the English throne was not seriously challenged in the reign of James I; no one disputed the fact that Government lay in the sovereign and his Council. The closest to a challenge came in the Form of Apology and Satisfaction [4.7] with its claim that the voice of the people was the voice of God. The assertion of the parliamentary privileges of free elections, free speech and freedom from arrest during a parliamentary session are recurring themes throughout the reign; that of free speech acquires increasing significance in the later Parliaments. Nevertheless, apart from the Addled Parliament, the Jacobean Parliaments completed a great deal of mundane business of essentially local interest. Even the Addled Parliament heard 105 bills introduced in the Commons in its two months of sitting!

4.1 James VI on monarchy, 1598

The kings … in Scotland were before any estates or ranks of men … before any parliaments were holden, or laws made: and by them was the land distributed (which at first was whole theirs) states erected … and forms of government devised and established: And so it follows of necessity that the kings were the authors and makers of the Laws, and not the laws of the kings …   5

And according to these fundamental Laws already alleged, we daily see that in the parliament (which is nothing else but the head court of the king and his vassals) the laws are but craved by his subjects, and only made by him at their rogation [request], and with their advice: For albeit the king make daily statutes and ordinances, enjoining such pains thereto as he thinks meet, without any advice of parliament or   10 estates; yet it lies in the power of no Parliament, to make any kind of Law or Statute without his sceptre be to it, for giving it the force of a Law …

For albeit it be true that the king is above the Law, as both the author and giver of strength thereto; yet a good king will not only delight to rule his subjects by the Law, but even will conform himself in his own actions thereunto, always keeping that   15 ground that the health of the commonwealth must be his chief Law.

James VI, *The Trew Law of Free Monarchies*, **1598, in** *Collected Works*, **1616, pp. 201ff.**

4.2 James VI on monarchy, 1599

For the part of making, and executing of Laws, consider first the trew difference betwixt a lawful good King; and a usurping Tyrant, and you shall the more easily understand your duty … The one acknowledges himself ordained for his people, having received from God a burden of government, whereof he must be accountable: the other thinks his people ordained for him, a prey to his passions and inordinate   5 appetites, as the fruits of his magnanimity: And therefore as their ends are directly contrary, so are their whole actions, as means, whereby they press to attain their ends. A good King, thinking his highest honour to consist in the due discharge of his calling, employs all his study and pains, to procure and maintain, by the making and execution of good Laws, the welfare and peace of his people … where by the   10 contrary, a usurping tyrant, thinking his greatest honour to consist in attaining … to his ambitious pretences, thinks himself never sure, but by dissections and factions among his people … And according to their actions, so they receive their reward: For a good King (after a happy and famous reign) dies in peace, lamented by his subjects, and admired by his neighbours; and leaving a reverent renown behind him on earth,   15 obtains the crown of eternal felicity in heaven …

Only remember, that as parliaments have been ordained for the making of laws, so do not abuse their institution, in holding them for any men's particulars …

James VI, *Basilikon Doron*, **1599, in** *Collected Works*, **p. 155**

4.3 A speech in Parliament, 1606

And as to the nature of this high Court of Parliament, it is nothing else but the
King's great Council, which the King assembles either upon occasion of interpreting,
or abrogating old Laws, or making of new … or for the public punishment of
notorious evil doers, or the praise and reward of virtuous and well deservers … It is
composed of a Head and a Body: the Head is the King, the Body are members of   5
Parliament. This body again is subdivided into two parts; the Upper and Lower
House.

… The life and strength of the Law consist not in heaving up infinite and confused
numbers of Laws, but in the right interpretation and good execution of good and
wholesome Laws. If this be so then, neither is this a place on the one side for every   10
rash and harebrained fellow to propone [propose] new Laws of his own invention …

James VI, *Collected Works*, pp. 506ff.

4.4 A speech to the Lords and Commons of the Parliament at Whitehall, 21 March 1610

The State of Monarchie is the supremest thing upon earth: For Kings are not only
God's Lieutenants upon earth, and sit upon God's throne, but even by God himself
they are called Gods … In the Scriptures Kings are called Gods, and so their power
after a certain relation compared to the Divine power. Kings are also compared to
Fathers of families: for a King is truly … the politic father of his people. And lastly,   5
Kings are compared to the head of this Microcosm of the body of man.

Kings are justly called Gods, for that they exercise a manner or resemblance of
Divine power upon earth. For if you will consider the Attributes to God, you shall
see how they agree in the person of a King. God hath power to create, or destroy,
make, or unmake at his pleasure, to give life, or send death, to judge all, and to be   10
judged nor accomptable to none: To raise low things, and to make high things low at
his pleasure, and to God are both soul and body due. And the like power have Kings:
they make and unmake their subjects: they have power of raising, and casting down:
of life, and of death: Judges over their subjects, like men at the Chess; a Pawn to take
a bishop or a Knight, and to cry up, or down any of their subjects, as they do their   15
money. And to the King is due both the affection of the soul, and the service of the
body of his subjects …

So in the first original of Kings, whereof some had their beginning by Conquest, and
some by election of the people, their wills at that time served for Law; Yet how soon
Kingdoms began to be settled in civilities and policy, then did Kings set down their   20
minds by Laws, which are properly made by the King only; but at the rogation of the
people, the King's grant being obtained thereunto. And so the King became to be
Lex loquens,[1] after a sort, binding himself by a double oath to the observation of the
fundamental Laws of his kingdom: Tacitly, as by being a King, and so bound to
protect as well the people, as the Laws of his Kingdom; And Expressly, by his oath at   25
his Coronation … And therefore a King governing in a settled Kingdom, leaves to be

a King and degenerates into a Tyrant, as soon as he leaves off to rule according to his Laws …

[1] Lex loquens = the law speaking

James VI, *Collected Works*, pp. 529ff.

Questions

1   The classic statements of James on monarchy [4.1, 4.2] were made shortly before 1603. What is the significance of the timing? Do you consider the statements to be good or bad public relations?
2   How does James justify his authority in 4.1, 4.2 and 4.4? Which of the justifications would he consider to be most valid?
3   What does the information in 4.1–4.4 contribute to your understanding of James's attitude to law?
4   How far, in the light of the above extracts, do you consider that James aimed to be an absolute ruler?
5   In what ways and to what extent does Rubens [1.21, 1.22] convey the image of the Divine Right of Kings in the Banqueting House ceiling?

The First Parliament 1604–11

4.5 A warrant from the speaker in relation to the case of Sir Thomas Shirley,[1] 22 March 1604

27 March 1604

This day the writ of habeas corpus[2] … for the bringing in of Sir Thomas Shirley, one of the members of the House and prisoner in the Fleet, was returned by the Warden of the Fleet, the prisoner himself brought to the Bar, and Simpson the goldsmith and Watkins the serjeant-at-mace as delinquents brought in by the Serjeant of the House …

Mr Speaker proposed divers questions to be answered by the said offenders: by whose relation it was averred that the writ was taken out on the thirtieth of January, was delivered to the serjeant the eleventh of February, before Sir Thomas was elected burgess; that Simpson and the serjeant, in the interim before the arrest, had no conference … one with the other; that the serjeant knew nothing at all of Sir Thomas's election, but understood by his Majesty's proclamation that no person outlawed for treason, felony, debt, or any other trespass, ought to be admitted a member of the Parliament, and was thereupon induced to think that Sir Thomas Shirley, standing outlawed, should not be elected or admitted a burgess, which if he had known or suspected, he would have been very careful not to have given offence to this honourable House by any such arrest.

To this Sir Thomas was admitted to answer, who affirmed that the arrest was made the fifteenth day of March, the day of his Majesty's first and solemn entrance through London, at what time he was going by commandment to wait upon his Majesty; whereof, upon the first offer to touch him, he wished the serjeant to take knowledge; as also that he was elected a burgess for the borough of Steyning in the   20
country of Sussex to serve at this present parliament; that, notwithstanding, they persisted in the arrest ...

The case being understood by the House, and the parties withdrawn, sundry learned members delivered their opinion, both in the point of privilege and in the point of law, for the state of the debt, the party being delivered out of execution by privilege ...

¹ Sir Thomas Shirley had been elected MP for Steyning but before the meeting of the Parliament in 1604 had been imprisoned for debt. The Commons took up his case as a question of privilege; the warden of the Fleet Prison refused to release him on the grounds that he would assume liability for Shirley's debts by releasing him. The Commons secured both the release of Shirley and an Act allowing creditors of MPs released on the grounds of privilege of Parliament to take out new writs against their debtors at the close of the Parliament.
² habeas corpus = a writ that safeguards the individual from arbitrary arrest by requiring just cause to be shown for the arrest. If this is shown, the individual then awaits trial; if just cause cannot be demonstrated, the prisoner must be released.

The Journal of the House of Commons, quoted in J. R. Tanner, *Constitutional Documents of the Reign of James I, 1603–1625*, 1961, p. 303

4.6 The Buckinghamshire election dispute: Goodwin v Fortescue¹

22 March 1604

The first motion was made ... on the behalf of Sir Francis Goodwin knight, who upon the first writ of summons directed to the Sheriff of Bucks was elected the first knight for the shire; but the return of his election being made, it was refused by the Clerk of the Crown quia utlagatus²: And because Sir John Fortescue, upon a second writ, was elected and entered in that place, his desire was that this return might be   5
examined and Sir Francis Goodwin received as a member of the House. The House gave way to the motion and, for a more debate and judicial proceeding in a case of privilege so important to the House, ordered that the Serjeant (the proper officer of the House) should give warning to the Clerk of the Crown to appear at the Bar³ at eight a clock the next morning, and to bring with him all the writs of summons,   10
indentures,⁴ and returns of elections for the County of Bucks ... for this Parliament: And to give warning to Sir Francis Goodwin to attend in person, whom their pleasure was to hear ...

23 March 1604

[After hearing the Clerk of the Crown and Sir Francis Goodwin, the discussion continued.]

In the meantime the whole case was at large opened and argued ... by sundry learned and grave members of the House, and after much dispute the question was agreed   15
upon and made: Whether Sir F. Goodwin were lawfully elected and returned one of the knights for Bucks, and ought to be admitted and received as a member of this House? Upon this question it was resolved in the affirmative ...

27 March 1604

Sir Edward Coke his Majesty's Attorney-General ... delivered from the Lords, That their Lordships taking notice in particular of the return of the Sheriff of Bucks and   20
acquainting his majesty with it, his Highness conceived himself engaged and touched in honour that there might be some conference of it between the two Houses; and to that end signified his pleasure unto them, and by them to this House.

Upon this message, so extraordinary and unexpected, the House entered into some consideration what were fit to be done; and resolved, That his majesty might be   25
moved for access the next day ...

29 March 1604

Mr Speaker relateth what he had delivered to the King by warrant from the House the day before ... His Majesty answered, he was loth he should be forced to alter his tune; and that he should now change it into matter of grief by way of contestation. He did sample [compare] it to the murmur and contradiction of the people of Israel   30
...

That he had no purpose to impeach their privilege; but since they derived all matters of privilege from him and by his grant, he expected they should not be turned against him ... By the law this House ought not to meddle with returns, being all made into the Chancery, and are to be corrected or reformed by that Court only into which they are returned ... That the Judges have now resolved that Sir Francis   35
Goodwin standeth outlawed according to the laws of this land ...

30 March 1604

Moved and, urged by one ... That now the case of Sir John Fortescue and Sir Francis Goodwin was become the case of the whole kingdom: That old lawyers forget, and commonly interpret the law according to the Time: that by this course, the free election of the country is taken away, and none shall be chosen, but such as   40
shall please the king and Council ...

5 April 1604

Mr Speaker ... bringeth message from his Majesty to this effect ... [that] he desired and commanded as an absolute King that there might be a conference between the House and the Judges; and that for that purpose there might be a select committee of

grave and learned persons out of the House; that his Council might be present, not 45
as umpires to determine, but to report indifferently on both sides.

Upon this unexpected message there grew some amazement, and silence: but at last
one stood up and said, The Prince's command is like a thunderbolt; his command
upon our allegiance like the roaring of a lion; to his command there is no
contradiction ... 50

Whereupon Mr Speaker proceeded to this Question: Whether to confer with the
Judges in the presence of the King and Council? Which was resolved in the
affirmative, and a select committee ... named ...

11 April 1604

... The King said ... That our privileges were not in question ... He granted that it
[the House] was a Court of record and a judge of returns. He moved that neither Sir 55
John Fortescue nor Sir Francis Goodwin might have place. Sir John losing his place,
his majesty did meet us half-way ...

So as the Question was presently made: Whether Sir John Fortescue and Sir Francis
Goodwin shall both be secluded, and a warrant for a new writ directed? And upon
the Question resolved, that a writ should issue for a new choice; and a warrant 60
directed accordingly ...

[1] The dispute arose from James's 1603 proclamation against the election of bankrupts or
outlaws to Parliament and the use of the Court of Chancery for the scrutiny of election
returns. The Buckinghamshire electors returned Sir Francis Goodwin, an outlaw. The Court
of Chancery declared his election null and void and issued a new writ for election in which the
government nominee Sir John Fortescue was returned. The commons insisted that Goodwin
had been wrongly described as an outlaw and asserted the right of the House to scrutinise
election returns. After long debates and considerable restraint on the part of James, a
compromise was reached by which James acknowledged that the House of Commons was a
court of record and a proper, although not sole, judge of election returns.
[2] quia utlagatus = because he was an outlaw
[3] Bar = a rail dividing the body of the House from a space where non Members may stand
when summoned
[4] indenture = a deed or contract between two parties, having the edges indented for
identification and security

The Journal of the House of Commons, quoted in Tanner, *Constitutional
Documents*, pp. 202–17

4.7 Form of Apology and Satisfaction, 20 June 1604[1]

To the King's most excellent Majesty: from the House of Commons assembled in
Parliament.

... What cause we your poor Commons have to watch over our privileges is manifest
in itself to all men. The prerogatives of princes may easily and do daily grow; the
privileges of the subject are for the most part at an everlasting stand. They may be by 5

good providence and care preserved, but being once lost are not recovered but with much disquiet ...

The rights of the liberties of the Commons of England consisteth chiefly in these three things:

First, That the shires, cities, and boroughs of England, by representation to be present, have free choice of such persons as they shall put in trust to represent them. 10

Secondly, That the persons chosen, during the time of the Parliament as also of their access and recess, be free from restraint, arrest, and imprisonment.

Thirdly, That in Parliament they may speak freely their consciences without check and controlment, doing the same with due reverence to the Sovereign Court of Parliament, that is, to your Majesty and both the Houses, who all in this case make but one politic body whereof your Highness is the Head. 15

These three several branches of the ancient inheritance of our liberty were in three matters ensuing apparently injured: the freedom of election in the case of Sir Francis Goodwin; the freedom of the persons elected in Sir Thomas Shirley's imprisonment; the freedom of our speech ... 20

For matter of religion ... your Majesty should be misinformed if any man should deliver that the Kings of England have any absolute power in themselves either to alter Religion (which God defend should be in the power of any mortal man whatsoever), or to make any laws concerning the same otherwise than as in temporal causes, by consent of Parliament ... We have not come in any Puritan or Brownist[2] spirit, to introduce their parity or to work the subversion of the state ecclesiastical as it now standeth ... Our desire hath also been to reform certain abuses crept into the ecclesiastical state even as into the temporal ... 25

[The Petition also raised issues of Assarts, or conversion of forests into arable land, and of wardship and other feudal 'burdens'.]

Let your Majesty be pleased to receive public information from your commons in Parliament as to the civil estate and government ... the voice of the people, in things of their knowledge, is said to be as the voice of God ... 30

[1] This document from the Committee to the House was never formally presented to James I.
[2] Brownists = followers of Thomas Browne, early Congregationalists

Peyt, *Jus Parliamentarium*, 1739, pp. 227–43, quoted in Tanner, *Constitutional Documents*, pp. 217–30

4.8 Dr Cowell's definition of king and prerogative[1]

KING ... He is above the law by his absolute power ... And though for the better and equal course in making laws he do admit the three estates, that is, Lords spiritual, Lords temporal, and the Commons unto counsel, yet this, in divers learned men's opinions, is not of constraint but out of his own benignity, or by reason of his promise made upon oath at the time of his coronation ... 5

PREROGATIVE OF THE KING ... is that especial power, preeminence, or privilege that the King hath in any kind over and above other persons, and above the ordinary course of the common law, in the right of his crown ... Only by the custom of this kingdom he maketh no laws without the consent of the three estates, though he may quash any law concluded of by them ... I hold it incontrovertible that the King of   10 England is an absolute King ...

Dr Cowell, *The Interpreter*, 1607, quoted in Tanner, *Constitutional Documents*, pp. 12–13

[1] Dr Cowell's book – a mixture of legal and constitutional dictionary and whatever else Cowell chose to define – outraged Parliament by the claims it made for the absolute authority of monarchy. James attempted to placate Parliament by agreeing to the banning of the book.

Questions

1   Why were the cases of Sir Thomas Shirley and Sir Francis Goodwin so enthusiastically pursued by the Commons in 1604?

2   How well did James I deal with these cases?

3   What evidence is there that the Form of Apology and Satisfaction reflected the concerns of some parliamentarians over the events at the Hampton Court Conference?

4   Using the above extracts and your own knowledge, to what extent had the Commons acquired the desire and capacity to obstruct Crown policies by 1607?

4.9 The power of the Crown in 1607 as perceived by the Venetian ambassador, Nicolo Molin, and reported to the Government of Venice

The Government is in the hands of the Council, who rule as the King desires; but occasion may arise where the public weal or ill is concerned, such as the introduction or the amendment of laws, supply, etc; in such cases the King ... is accustomed to continue the old practice and to summon Parliament in its three Estates of the Realm, the clergy, Nobility and Commons. It cannot be denied that originally and for   5 many years later the authority of members was great, for each one was permitted, without fear of punishment, to speak his mind freely on all that concerned the State ... But now that the Sovereign is absolute, matters move in a very different fashion ... Parliament can pass no law, nay, may not even assemble without the royal consent. The Crown, too, by various means, secures the exclusion of those whom it does not   10 like and the inclusion of those upon whose support it thinks it may count. The Sovereign has now reached such a pitch of formidable power that he can do what he likes, and there is no one who would dare either in Parliament or out of it, except at the grave risk of ruin ...

It is true that the present King, who came to the throne as quietly as could possibly   15 be desired, wishing to show his gratitude to his subjects, announced that he intended

to leave the elections free ... But he presently repented and saw that the course
pursued by his predecessors was the true one. For in the Lower House were some
members who, moved by public zeal or private interest or a blend of both,
persistently opposed all his demands ... This was the cause of the opposition to the   20
Union and of the difficulties in the way of subsidies. The latter he overcame, not
through the goodwill of Parliament, but through their pockets; for he gave out that
unless the subsidy was voted he would be unable to repay the money he had
borrowed.

Calendar of State Papers Venetian, vol. 10, p. 509

4.10 Assertion of parliamentary privilege, 1610[1]

First, we hold it an ancient, general, and undoubted right of parliament, to debate
freely, all matters which do properly concern the Subject, and his Right or State;
which Freedom of Debate being once foreclosed, the essence of the liberty of
Parliament is withal dissolved.

Journal of the House of Commons, vol. 1, p. 431

[1] This prefaced a request for a full inquiry and examination of impositions.

4.11 The king's letter to the Privy Council, December 1610

[We] are sure no House save the House of Hell could have found so many
[complaints] as they have already done ... [We] are sorry of our ill fortune in this
country, that having lived so long as we did in the kingdom where we were born, we
came out of it with an unstained reputation and without any grudge in the people's
hearts but for wanting of us. Wherein we have misbehaved ourself here we know not,   5
nor we can never yet learn ... Our fame and actions have been daily tossed like tennis
balls amongst them and all that spite and malice durst do to disgrace ... us hath been
used. To be short, this Lower House by their behaviour have imperilled and annoyed
our health, wounded our reputation, emboldened all ill-natured people, encroached
upon many of our privileges, and plagued our purse with their delays.

The Letters of King James VI and I, ed. G. P. V. Akrigg, 1984, no. 150

Questions

1   How successfully had Parliament established its privileges during the
    First Parliament?
2   With what justification might James I have regarded the Commons as
    'the House of Hell' [4.11, line 1] during the years of the First
    Parliament? (Consider the obstructive attitude towards royal finances.)
3   How does James in 1610 [4.11] refute the picture of his authority painted
    by the Venetian ambassador [4.9]?

The Addled Parliament, 5 April to 7 June 1614

This Parliament was called to provide subsidies. It proved reluctant to do so until grievances were redressed. The dynamics of faction and the determination of the Commons to discuss impositions and criticise favourites, made cooperation between Crown and Parliament impossible in the addled, or confused Parliament.

4.12 From the king's speech to both Houses, 5 April 1614

Although there have been many speeches given abroad that the King would stretch his prerogative, like other of my predecessors, I never meant it. For he that overmuch strains and blows his nose will cause much blood. So, if a prince should stretch his prerogative, it would cause his people to bleed.

It is reported, I am sure, amongst [you] that there should be some that should be   5
undertakers for me and that the King should have a packed parliament. Whosoever should think so I should count him a traitor. I assure you there is no such thing, for whosoever should do this I should count him a knave and you might account me a fool. The only thing [that was told me] (which every good subject would do the like) was this: that talking with some of the Upper House and others that wait upon me   10
they did assure me that I had no reason to doubt but that the people, knowing my necessity, would willingly contribute to relieve me and to pay my debts.

Journal of the House of Commons, **quoted in M. Jansson (ed.),** *Proceedings in Parliament (House of Commons), 1614*, 1988, p. 17

4.13 The 1614 Parliament as seen in the correspondence of John Chamberlain to Sir Dudley Carleton, April 1614

7 April

The Returns of the Knights from divers Shires proves every day more litigious.

14 April

... The King made a Speech to the whole Assembly in the Great Banqueting-chamber, wherein he laid out his wants, and descended as it were to entreating to be relieved, and that they would show their good affection toward him in such sort, that this Parliament might be called 'The Parliament of Love'.   5

3 May

The King hath a great deal of patience [with the Parliament] ... And indeed I would wish they would not stand too stiff, but take some moderate course to supply him by ordinary means, lest he be driven to ways of worse consequence, wherein he shall not want colour both from the law and pulpit.

9 June

While the Parliament grew every day more fiery and violent in their Speeches, the   10
King sent them a Letter … whereby he signified unto them, that … he meant to
dissolve the Parliament, unless in the meantime they fell roundly in hand to consider
and provide how to relieve his wants; neither would he expect or receive other answer
from them than the speedy effecting of this business. This peremptory message
wrought diversely with them, and made some of them put water into their wine,   15
seeing the time of their reign so near an end. But the greater part grew more averse,
and would not descend to so sudden a resolution … Whereby this Meeting or
Assembly is to be held a blank Parliament, or rather parley, not having so much as the
name of a Session, but, as the words went, Parliamentum inchoatum.[1]

[1] Parliamentum inchoatum = confused or addled Parliament

J. Nichols, *The Progresses of James I*, 1828, vol. 3, pp. 3–4

4.14 Sir Francis Bacon's speech concerning the undertakers, 1614

I have been hitherto silent in this matter of Undertaking, wherein, as I perceive, the
House is much enwrapped.

First, because (to be plain with you) I did not well understand what it meant, or what
it was … That private men should undertake for the commons of England! Why, a
man might as well undertake for the four elements. It is a thing so giddy, and so vast,   5
as cannot enter into the brain of a sober man. And specially in a new Parliament;
when it was impossible to know who should be of the Parliament: and when all men,
that know never so little the constitution of this House, do know it to be so open to
reason, as men do not know when they enter into these doors what mind themselves
will be of, until they hear things argued and debated … I think Aesop was a wise   10
man, that described the nature of a fly that sat upon the spoke of the chariot wheel
and said to herself, 'What a dust do I raise?' So, for my part, I think that all this dust
is raised by light rumours and buzzes, and not upon any solid ground.

Works of Francis Bacon, ed. James Spedding, vol. 14, 1874, pp. 42–45

4.15 Bishop Neile of Lincoln's speech in the Lords, 24 May 1614

My Lords, I think it a dangerous thing for us to confer with them about the point of
impositions. For it is a Noli me tangere,[1] and none that have either taken the Oath
of Supremacy or Allegiance may do it with good conscience, for in the Oath of
Allegiance we are sworn to maintain the privileges of the Crown, and in this conference we should not confer about a flower, but strike at the root of the Imperial   5
Crown, and therefore in my opinion it is neither fit to confer with them nor give
them a meeting.

[1] Noli me tangere = not to be touched upon

T. L. Moir, *The Addled Parliament of 1614*, 1958, p. 117

4.16 Report of a committee on Bishop Neile's speech

Bishop's scandalous assertions: He maintained that the matter of impositions, to dispute of them in the Lower House was noli me tangere. That whosoever has taken the oath of allegiance may not dispute the King's prerogative, for it strikes at the root and imperial crown. And dissuaded for conference with the lower House, for he affirmed that the spirits of the lower House would be undutiful and seditious.

M. Jansson, *Proceedings in Parliament (House of Commons), 1614*, 1988, p. 363

Questions

1   In what ways does Sir Francis Bacon in **4.14** support James I's denial in **4.12** of the use of undertakers and of attempts to pack the 1614 Parliament?

2   What, according to **4.12**, were James's objectives in summoning Parliament in 1614? How does the writer of **4.13** indicate his attitude to the predicament of the king?

3   Why were impositions such an important issue in 1614? Why was Bishop Neile's speech so inflammatory [**4.15, 4.16**]?

The Third Parliament, 30 January 1621 to 6 January 1622

King James summoned his Third Parliament in the wake of the outbreak of the Thirty Years War, his son-in-law's loss of the Palatinate as well as Bohemia, declining trade following the disastrous Cockayne Project,[1] and deteriorating Crown finances [**5.26–5.30**]. The parliamentary agenda focused on the abuse of monopolies, seen as central to the decline in commerce, and the need to support the Protestant cause in Europe. The increasing prominence of Villiers and his clan at court made matters involving patronage even more sensitive. While the monopolies debates and the revival of impeachment for Mompesson and Bacon – a servant of the Crown – dominated the Commons, the highlight of the 1621 Parliament was a series of exchanges between the king and the Commons on the nature of privilege, especially that of free speech. In January 1622 relations between them were ruptured in a dramatic manner as King James ripped the Protestation from the Commons

[1] In 1614 Alderman Cockayne gained royal approval for his project to export finished cloth. The monopoly granted to Cockayne and his company not only damaged the interests of the Merchant Adventurers but provoked a hostile reaction from the Dutch, who resented the loss of their privilege to import unfinished English cloth and banned the import of English finished cloth. Cockayne's monopoly was ended in 1617. It contributed to a slump in the cloth trade that was felt for a number of years and caused many complaints from those involved in textiles.

Journal, leaving some contemporaries convinced that he would never again call Parliament and would seek to resolve the problem of the Palatinate by a Spanish marriage for Prince Charles.

4.17 The king's speech to Parliament, 30 January 1621

First, as in all parliaments, it is the king's office to care and procure the making of good laws ... The second cause of the calling of this parliament was the cause of religion in general ... As concerning the match with Spain, whereas it hath been thought that I should grow cold in religion and suffer the papists to triumph over us, I will say this, that I would never speak anything in private which I would not have to be known in public. And whatever I have treated of about that match, if it had not tended to the furtherance of religion, I am not worthy to be your king. 5

The main errand why this parliament is called ... is for to sustain me in my urgent necessity ... No man within my dominions can complain of poverty which is not through his own default; that either he doth not work or lives unthrifty ... I have had less supply from my people than ever king or queen had, I know not for how many hundred years ... I have laboured as a woman in travail, not ten months but ten years, for within that time have I not had a parliament or a subsidy. And I dare say I have been as sparing to trouble you not with monopolies ... 10

The next cause of calling this parliament is one particular urgent necessity, which is the miserable spectacle that no man can look upon without a weeping eye ... The Palatinate invaded, which I so laboured to prevent ... and now I am to provide for wars that my son in law may be restored to those his ancient possessions which are yet lost; and nothing can be expected from you without begging as a man would beg an alms ... For I declare it unto you that if I cannot get it with peace, my crown and my blood and the blood of my son shall not be spared for it. But I can do nothing without sustenance from my people; and never King of England had less supply than I have had, considering these extraordinary occasions heretofore mentioned ... 15

20

But you of the Lower House, I would not have you to meddle with complaints against the King, the church or state matters, nor with princes' prerogatives. The parliament was never called for that purpose. And if among you there be any such busy body, he is a spirit of Satan that means to overthrow the good errand in hand ... 25

The Commons Debates 1621 , ed. W. Notestein, F. H. Relf and H. Simpson, vol. 2, pp. 1ff.

Questions

1   What, according to the king's speech, were the main issues to be addressed in 1621?
2   Why was finance the key factor in the calling of this Parliament?
3   In what ways do you detect the influence of Lionel Cranfield in source **4.17** (see also **5.30**)?

4.18 The king's statement on the question of free speech, 15 February 1621

Mr Secretary Calvert said that the King had commanded him to tell the House from his majesty that he gave as free liberty to speak as any king before him ever did and if any speak otherwise than they ought he hoped that the House would see them punished there.

This gave good satisfaction to the House but they desired Mr Secretary would set   5
down the very words in the Clerk's book ... The words in effect were these: That his Majesty did grant liberty and freedom of speech in as ample manner as ever any of his predecessors ever did and if any should speak undutifully (as he hoped none would) he doubted not but we ourselves would be more forward to punish it than to require it; and he willed us to rest satisfied with this rather than to trouble him with   10
any petition or message and so cast ourselves upon one of these rocks, that if we asked for too little we should wrong ourselves, if too much or more than right he would be forced to deny us which he would be very loath to do.

Notestein, Relf and Simpson, *The Commons Debates*, vol. 2, pp. 83–84

4.19 The king's speech to the House at Whitehall, 20 April 1621

That I have been strangely exhausted of my means you all know ... Yet my son in law and grandchildren are out of all, and though ... I hope to help them by a treaty, yet do I leave nothing undone which is fit for preparation. I have bestowed £18,000 in arms. Besides, my son (in law) has five children and I am forced to maintain them. My ambassador is to go again to the Archduke and from thence round about into   5
Spain, which will be a great charge unto me ...

Notestein, Relf and Simpson, *The Commons Debates*, vol. 2, p. 303

4.20 Foreign affairs: debates in the House, 3 December 1621

Sir Edward Sackville took exception to that part of the petition wherein it is desired that the prince might be married to one of his own religion ... We have been careful all this parliament not to touch the King's prerogative but what greater prerogative is there than to make war, matches and alliance. By pressing the King hereunto either he must forego his own ways and ends or deny the petition of the commonwealth.   5
What need we to touch this considering we have a prince that anticipates time. He is but young in years but old in judgment. And shall we think that whomsoever he shall marry that he will alter his religion? Or should we not think he will rather convert her than she him?...

Sir Richard Weston, Chancellor of the Exchequer, said we will not meddle with the   10
marriage for as princes do best when they take counsel of this House so we ought not to speak of what will not be heard ... it's good when the king adviseth with his parliament of war but for the parliament to advise the king of war is presumptuous
...

Mr Wentworth. ... There is a relation of the Gunpowder Treason; I wish it may be
read, for these walls (methinks) do yet shake at it. And I would know whether those   15
36 barrels of gunpowder under these walls do not require this? ... Methinks it
would be suitable to petition God's lieutenant ... The king is never greater than
in parliament, and we can never approach more nearly to our head than there ...

Sir George More. The institution of a parliament is to present grievances to the king.
Now the greatest grievance we have is the decay of true religion and here to open the   20
insolencies of popish recusants. And in this if we should not deal plainly, we should
not deal faithfully. Moreover, by connivance they will increase and grow in number
and arrogancy.

Sir Robert Phelips. If I thought this petition would be offensive to the King I would
not have it spoken of. If I thought it would make a breach upon his Majesty's reason,   25
affection or power, I would first bid away with it. But it will not, for his Majesty at a
close of his speech at Whitehall bad us speak freely unto him, Wherefore I dare be
bold to say that in the match with Spain there is neither honour, profit not safety.

Sir Edward Coke ... Marriage and leagues, war and peace, they are arcana imperii[1]
and not to be meddled with. If they were a petition of right that required an answer,   30
I would never prefer it or give my consent to the preferring of it; but it is only a
petition of grace ... [We] desire that we might fight against Spain. We say that the
hope of the marriage with Spain is the cause of the insolency of the papists. We
advise nothing but what his Majesty liketh, for surely it will avert the hearts of many
that he should marry with any but a protestant ... To do this by way of petition is   35
good and hath no hurt in it ...

[1] arcana imperii = mysteries of state

Notestein, Relf and Simpson, *The Commons Debates,* **vol. 2, pp. 487ff.**

Questions

1   Compare the arguments advanced for and against the Spanish marriage
    in **4.20**. In what ways might this marriage have proved a good solution
    for James's diplomatic dilemma in 1621?
2   Why was anti-Catholicism so virulent in 1621 [**3.29, 6.10–6.14**]?
3   On what grounds did Sir Edward Coke in **4.20** recommend a petition to
    the king?

4.21 The Commons Petition, 3 December 1621

1   That seeing this inevitable necessity is fallen upon your Majesty ... your Majesty
    would not omit this just occasion speedily and effectually to take your sword into
    your hand.
2   ... [That] your Majesty would resolve to pursue and more publicly avow the
    aiding of those of our religion in foreign parts ...   5
    ...

4 That the bent of this war and point of your sword may be against that prince ...
whose armies and treasures have first diverted and since maintained the war in the
Palatinate.

5 ... [And] to put into execution ... the laws already and hereafter to be made for
preventing of dangers by Popish recusants and their wonted evasions.   10

6 That to frustrate their hopes for a future age, our most noble Prince may be
timely and happily married to one of our own religion.

This is the sum and effect of our humble declaration, which we (no ways intending
to press upon your Majesty's undoubted and regal prerogative) do with the fullness
of our duty and obedience humbly submit to your most princely consideration.

J. Rushworth, *Historical Collections*, 1659, vol. 1, p. 40, quoted in Tanner,
***Constitutional Documents*, pp. 276ff.**

4.22 The king's letter to the Commons, 3 December 1621

We have heard by divers reports, to our great grief, that our distance from the
Houses of Parliament caused by our indisposition of health hath emboldened some
fiery and popular spirits of some of the House of Commons to argue and debate
publicly of the matters far above their reach and capacity, tending to our high
dishonour and breach of prerogative royal. These are therefore to command you   5
to make known in our name unto the House, that none therein shall presume
henceforth to meddle with anything concerning our government or deep matters
of State, and namely not to deal with our dearest son's match with the daughter
of Spain, nor to touch the honour of that King or any other our friends and
confederates ... [We] think ourself very free and able to punish any man's   10
misdemeanours in Parliament, as well during their sitting as after ...

Rushworth, *Historical Collections*, vol. 1, p. 43, quoted in Tanner,
***Constitutional Documents*, p. 279**

4.23 The Commons Petition, 9 December 1621

... And whereas your Majesty doth seem to abridge us of the ancient liberty of
parliament for freedom of speech, jurisdiction, and just censure of the House, and
other proceedings there (wherein we trust in God we shall never transgress the
bounds of loyal and dutiful subjects), a liberty which we assure ourselves so wise and
so just a king will not infringe, the same being our ancient and undoubted right, and   5
an inheritance received from our ancestors; without which we cannot freely debate
nor clearly discern of things in question before us ...

Rushworth, *Historical Collections*, vol. 1, p. 46, quoted in Tanner,
***Constitutional Documents*, p. 282**

4.24 The king's letter, Newmarket, 11 December 1621

… In the body of your petition you usurp upon our prerogative royal, and meddle
with things far above your reach, and then in the conclusion you protest the
contrary; as if a robber would take a man's purse and then protest he meant not to
rob him. For first, you presume to give us your advice concerning the match of our
dearest son with some Protestant (we cannot say princess, for we know none of these   5
fit for him) and dissuade us from his match with Spain, urging us to a present war
with that king; and yet in the conclusion, forsooth, ye protest ye intend not to press
upon our most undoubted and regal prerogative, as if the petitioning of us in matters
that yourselves confess ye ought not to meddle with were not a meddling with them
…

And although we cannot allow of the style, calling it 'your ancient and undoubted   10
right and inheritance', but could rather have wished that ye had said that your
privileges were derived from the grace and permission of our ancestors and us … yet
we are pleased to give you our royal assurance that as long as you contain yourselves
within the limits of your duty, we will be as careful to maintain and preserve your
lawful liberties and privileges as ever any of our predecessors were, nay, as to preserve   15
our own royal prerogative. So as your House shall only have need to beware to trench
upon the prerogative of the Crown; which would enforce us, or any just king, to
retrench them of their privileges that would pare his prerogative and flowers of the
Crown …

Rushworth, *Historical Collections*, vol. 1, pp. 46–52, quoted in Tanner,
Constitutional Documents, pp. 283–87

4.25 The Commons' Protestation, 18 December 1621

The Commons now assembled in Parliament … do make this Protestation following,
That the liberties, franchises, privileges, and jurisdiction of Parliament are the
ancient and undoubted birthright and inheritance of the subjects of England; and
that the arduous and urgent affairs concerning the King, State, and defence of the
realm and of the Church of England, and the maintenance and making of laws, and   5
redress of mischiefs and grievances which daily happen within this realm, are proper
subjects and matter of counsel and debate in Parliament … and that the Commons in
Parliament have like liberty and freedom of speech to propound, treat, reason, and
bring to conclusion the same … and that every member of the said House hath like
freedom from all impeachment, imprisonment, and molestation (other than by   10
censure of the House itself) for or concerning any speaking, reasoning, or declaring
of any matter or matters touching the Parliament or Parliament business …

Rushworth, *Historical Collections*, vol. 1 , p. 53, quoted in Tanner,
Constitutional Documents, p. 288

Questions

1 What are the key issues in dispute between James and Parliament in the exchanges reported in **4.17–4.25**?
2 How far do they represent deep-seated issues rather than immediate problems of the years 1621–22?
3 How strong is the argument that such issues would not have been voiced had it not been for a fundamentally flawed plan of dynastic marriages?
4 Did James make any real concessions to Parliament as a result of the Third Parliament? To what extent had Parliament gained the initiative in its relations with the Crown by 1622?

The Fourth Parliament, 19 February 1624 to 27 March 1625

After the dissolution of the Third Parliament James relied on the Spanish marriage as the tool to restore the Palatinate to his son-in-law. The failure of Prince Charles and Buckingham to secure that marriage by the 1623 visit to Madrid **[6.10]** guaranteed a Parliament superficially keen for war with Spain in 1624. Still reluctant to agree to war, James unequivocally invited the advice of Parliament **[4.26]**. Cranfield was sacrificed to his parliamentary enemies for his attempts to secure the ousting of Buckingham and his opposition to war on financial grounds. His impeachment illustrated the potential of that device for removing royal ministers. The Monopolies Act of 1624 was a sop to gain subsidies for war **[5.32]** and the subsidies voted were to be appropriated and administered by a committee chosen by the Commons to guard against abuse. Mansfeld's expedition to relieve the Palatinate was raised in November 1624 and became the first of a series of disasters during the reign of Charles I. The Fourth Parliament ended with the death of James in 1625.

4.26 The king's speech at the opening of Parliament, 19 February 1624

I have been these many years upon treaties; but so far as I thought … for settling a peace in Christendom, and settling of peace at home. And in these treaties I went long on, but finding in them a slower success than I expected, or had reason to do, I was willing, and especially in one thing concerning the estate of my grandchildren, to see a good and speedy end. And in this finding as great promises as I could wish, and   5 yet finding their actions clean contrary, it stirred up my son to offer himself to make that journey, and I thank God, having him here now, I have no cause to repent it; for, being of fit age and ripeness for marriage, he urged me to know the certainty in a matter of so great weight, that he might not be put off with long delays, for delay in such case is more dangerous than denial … [And] with him I only sent the man   10 whom I most trusted, Buckingham, commanding him never to leave him, nor return home without him ... I had general hopes before, but particulars will resolve matters, generals will not, and before this journey things came to me as raw, as if I had never treated of therefore; and I was as far disappointed of my ends as if I had been wakened out of a dream. Now I have put it into certainty, and whereas I walked in a   15 mist before I have now brought it to particulars ... And, when you have heard all ... I shall entreat your good and sound advice, for the glory of God, the peace of the kingdom, and the weal of my children. Never king gave more trust to his subjects than to desire their advice in matters of this weight, for I assure you ye may freely advise me, seeing, of my princely fidelity, ye are entreated therunto ...

J. P. Kenyon, *The Stuart Constitution*, 1966, p. 48

4.27 Alvise Valaresso, Venetian ambassador in England, reporting on the fall of Cranfield, 26 April 1624

Parliament is all intent in debating and settling the case of the Lord Treasurer; his misdemeanours are varied, but the chief are receiving bribes in the administration of his office and imposing charges of his own authority. He deserves ill as he certainly had Spanish sympathies. The action of enquiring and proceeding against him is good, but the time is perhaps unfortunate and the delay certainly harmful. The   5 objects of the inquiry differ with different people. Some act for the punishment of guilt; some to abase a Spanish partisan; some from desire of change; some to profit by the confiscation of his goods to use them for public purposes; and all are moved by his universal unpopularity, as being a man of low birth and raised by the king's favour to the dignities of treasurer and an earldom, he has behaved very haughtily in   10 the latter and proved very stingy in making payments in the former. The Prince and Buckingham are his chief enemies, the latter of long standing through some offence, and more recently from refusing money he required and opposing him although he was the duke's creation and a near relation, and because quite recently he brought forward the youth Brent ... with the idea of winning the king's favour and ousting   15 Buckingham. Although he was not a bad minister to the king, and is thought to have presumed somewhat upon his support, his Majesty cares nothing about and abandons him to the pleasure and justice of parliament ... Thus the energies and abilities of the parliament are involved in what one may call a private affair while the more important public resolutions are delayed and suspended.

Cal State Papers Venetian, vol. 18, pp. 278–79

Questions

1   How tenable is the view that James I had lost interest in affairs of State by 1624?
2   How much initiative lay with Parliament by 1624?
3   What evidence is there in **4.27** that James I was using the fall of Cranfield (see Chapter 5) to play for time?

4   What conclusions can be drawn on the importance of faction at the court from the career and fall of Cranfield (see also **5.25, 5.30**)?

Recommended reading

R. Cust and A. Hughes (eds.), *Conflict in Early Stuart England*, 1989

J. Daly, 'The idea of absolute monarchy in seventeenth century England', *Historical Journal*, vol. 21, 1978

E. R. Foster (ed.), *Proceedings in Parliament 1610*, vols. 1 and 2, 1966

J. H. Hexter (ed.), *Parliament and Liberty*, 1992

M. Jansson (ed.), *Proceedings in Parliament, 1614, The House of Commons*, 1988

T. L. Moir, *The Addled Parliament of 1614*, 1958

R. C. Munden, 'The defeat of Sir John Fortescue: court and country at the hustings', *English Historical Review* , vol. 93, 1978

W. Notestein, *The House of Commons 1604–1610*, 1971

L. L. Peck (ed.), *The Mental World of the Jacobean Court*, 1991

R. E. Ruigh, *The Parliament of 1624*, 1971

C. Russell, *Parliaments and English Politics*, 1979

K Sharpe (ed.), *Faction and Parliament*, 1973

D. Starkey (ed.), *The English Court from the Wars of the Roses to the Civil War*, 1987

J. P. Somerville, *Politics and Ideology in England, 1603–1640*, 1986

H. Tomlinson (ed.), *Before the English Civil War*, 1983

R. B. Zaller, *The Parliament of 1621: A Study in Constitutional Conflict*, 1971

5 'He was very liberal of what he had not in his own grip.' The financial problems of James I

Time chart	
1603	James inherited a debt of £422,000
1604	Grievances of wardship and purveyance raised in Parliament Great Farm of the Customs Treaty of London ended the war with Spain
1606	Bate's case
1608	Cecil became Lord Treasurer Revised Book of Rates Extension of impositions
1610	Failure of the Great Contract
1611	Sale of baronetcies began Retrenchment and augmentation of prerogative taxation
1612	Death of Cecil
1613	Funeral expenses following the death of Prince Henry Wedding expenses for the marriage of Princess Elizabeth
1614	Attack on impositions in the Addled Parliament Cockayne Project
1616	Sale of the Cautionary Towns to the Dutch
1618	Outbreak of the Thirty Years War Trade depression
1619	Funeral expenses following the death of Queen Anne
1621	Attack on monopolists Impeachment of Bacon Inadequate war subsidies offered Cranfield became Lord Treasurer
1624	Impeachment of Cranfield Monopolies Act Subsidy Act

However much the reputation of James I has been 'revised' and his statecraft vindicated, it is very difficult to whitewash his financial incompetence. His financial simplicity is well attested [1.1, 1.4] and he perceived impecuniousness as the one flaw in his happiness [5.1, 5.8]. It may be asked whether the financial problems of the king were of his own making or part of the *damnosa hereditas* (cursed legacy) of Elizabeth. He inherited a ramshackle financial system; he had few financial skills. The financial situation was complex and changing. The expenditure of the Government was increasing and inflation was beginning to bite. Peace, retrenchment and reform were the bare essentials of solvency; good overseas trade and the cooperation of Parliament in a radical overhaul of the system were required for lasting success. James's financial advisers succeeded in little more than superficial measures; in many cases, for example impositions [5.14–5.16], the remedies had consequences that were far-reaching and undesirable. No merchant wanted additional levies to be imposed over and above the normal customs schedules, especially as these were added by virtue of royal prerogative. John Bate's refusal to pay impositions in 1606 enabled James to secure the backing of the Court of the Exchequer for impositions. This verdict gnawed at Crown–Parliament relations well into the reign of his son.

The reign divides into two periods as far as finance is concerned: that dominated by Robert Cecil, Earl of Salisbury, lasting from the beginning of the reign until the death of Cecil in 1612; the post-Cecil era was eventually dominated by Lionel Cranfield, Earl of Middlesex, who struggled against court extravagance, a trade depression and the financial implications of impending war, before falling victim to court faction in 1624.

The reign began with a debt of £422,000 and certain unavoidable problems. Increased court expenditure was necessary: James had his own court; there was also that of the queen and after 1610 that of the Prince of Wales. The size of the court increased the demands on purveyance, already an unpopular feudal device [5.13] by which the purveyor, a court officer, was able to secure food and carriages for the court at a fraction of the market price. As a 'foreign' king he had also to be seen to be generous in rewarding Crown servants with pensions and annuities, leases on Crown lands, tax farms, monopolies and wardships. (Unpopular and feudal in origin, wardships placed heirs of tenants-in-chief who were minors in wardship to the king until they came of age. During the period of wardship the king administered their estates [5.12].) Unfortunately some of these rewards were doubly counter-productive, enriching Scottish sycophants to the distaste of the English and raising expectations of more to come. The patronage system blocked the necessary radical solution; the king's impecuniousness prevented the buying-out of corrupt office holders.

In short, an extravagant king [5.4–5.9] operated a financial system where the Crown's revenue was dependent on income from customs duties (often via tax farmers), Crown lands (whose rents were declining), fines from the prerogative courts (an erratic source), income from the feudal fiscal prerogatives (unpopular) and subsidies from unwilling Parliaments [5.11, 5.29]. Even the union with Scotland [5.3, 5.12] was used against him in matters of finance: it was argued that union should bring about a reduction in burdens and the king should remember the frugal ways of ruling Scotland. There is an argument for saying that the financial situation was not entirely hopeless. Much of the 1601 subsidy granted to Elizabeth had not been collected, the Crown could justify a revision of Customs (last reviewed in 1558), and a reassessment of the value of Crown lands was called for. Furthermore, the great drains on Elizabeth's coffers (the Spanish War and the Irish campaigns) had ground to a halt by 1603. The Treaty of London with Spain not only removed a burden but promised an increase in wealth through the extension of trade into the Spanish European possessions. The union removed the need for an expensive garrison at Berwick.

After the early years of lack-lustre administration by Dorset [5.17, 5.18], Cecil [5.19, 5.20] assumed direct control of the Treasury in 1608 and worked well with Caesar to devise methods that would augment revenue. The Revised Book of Rates of 1608 promised to increase revenue by £70,000 but proved unpopular with merchants. Impositions ensured that the king benefited from the improvement in trade, but they also created the atmosphere in the 1610 session whereby acceptance of the one hope for the salvation of James's finances, the Great Contract, floundered in a sea of mutual suspicion between king and Parliament. Its timing was no accident. Pauline Croft's research on Cecil has shown the great significance Cecil attached to Prince Henry becoming Prince of Wales in that year. Cecil feared that Henry would exercise lavish patronage at home and seek expensive intervention for Protestantism abroad. This argued for an effective parliamentary settlement with James I in 1610 – the Great Contract. This was the high point of the Cecil era; its failure [5.21–5.23] left the monarchy wide open to severe pressures. Endemic inefficiency and corruption, together with inertia and the king's punctilious regard for his 'honour', minimised the efforts of his loyal servants. Danger signs were evident at the outset and the king never seriously tackled the problem of his own attitude.

James I's attitude to finance

5.1 King James to Viscount Cranborne (Robert Cecil), 1604

... I cannot but confess that it is an horror to me to think upon the height of my place, the greatness of my debts and smallness of my means. It is true my 'hairte' is greater than my rent, and my care to preserve my honour and credit by payment of my debts far greater than my possibility.

Historical Manuscripts Commission, *Calendar of the Manuscripts of the Most Honourable The Marquess of Salisbury*, ed. M. S. Giuseppi, 1933, p. 394

5.2 Insights into James's approach to finance

5.2(a)

In experience it is good to be neither pinching nor prodigal, yet if means allow it, rather thought a little profuse than too sparing ...

5.2(b)

It much conduces to the public weal, either of a Principality, or republic, not to suffer the money and treasure of a state to be ingrossed into the hands of few: money is like muck, not good unless it be spread.

Regales Aphorismi or A Royal Chain of Golden Sentences ... Delivered by King James. Collected by Certain Reverend and Honourable Personages Attending on his Majesty, 1650, no. 83, p. 44, and no. 224, p. 112

5.3 A Letter from Matthew Hutton, Archbishop of York, to Lord Cecil, 10 August 1604

His Majesty's subjects hear and fear that his excellent and heroical nature is too much inclined to giving, which in short will exhaust the treasure of this kingdom and bring many inconveniences. His Majesty in Scotland lived like a noble and worthy king of small revenues in comparison, because he wisely foresaw that expensae[1] should not exceed recepta;[2] which I fear his Highness does not in England but not   5 minding his yearly recepta and recipienda[3] (though great, yet not infinite) yields almost to every man's petition. If this should continue this kingdom will not serve, but that his Majesty contrary to his princely nature must be compelled to be burdenous and grievous to his most loyal and obedient subjects.

[1] expensae = expenses
[2] recepta = income
[3] recipienda = dues, amounts due to him

Historical Manuscripts Commission, *Calendar of the Manuscripts of the Most Honourable The Marquess of Salisbury*, p. 220

Questions

1   In spite of regarding England as a land flowing with milk and honey, James had some appreciation of his lack of revenue. How does the evidence [5.1–5.3] suggest that James subordinated the pursuit of thrift to the desire for promoting his image?

2   Why does the Archbishop of York use the Scottish example in his letter to Cecil?

3   What is the meaning and significance of the phrase 'his Majesty … must be compelled to be burdenous and grievous to his most loyal and obedient servants' [5.3, lines 8–9]?

4   What are the apparent financial weaknesses of James I at the beginning of the reign? How might he avoid further financial difficulties?

Peace with Spain in 1604 offered a step towards solvency but a coherent policy of retrenchment did not follow. Court extravagance continued.

5.4 Draft letter from the Council to the king, December 1604

… We perceive your Majesty had no purpose to give cause of any such charges at this time, but only wished some masque[1] might be thought on (at such a festival time) … Wherein though we concur so far, yet because we find, how justly you judge of those that wish your estate to be more safe by stay of expense, than it is in respect of your great necessities, we are bold to let your Majesty know how many Christmases pass   5 without any such note; dancing, comedies, plays, and other such sports having been thought sufficient marks of mirth, except some great strange prince or extraordinary marriages fell in that time.

[1] masques = entertainments on special occasions that combined theatre, music and dancing. They were very popular at the early Stuart court, where many masques were written by Ben Jonson and staged by Inigo Jones.

Historical Manuscripts Commission, *Calendar of the Manuscripts of the Most Honourable The Marquess of Salisbury,* p. 388

5.5 A letter from Sir Thomas Lake on a court masque for James I, 27 November 1607

His highness commanded me further to advertise your lordship that where he had by my former brief sent your lordship a warrant for a masque with a blank but limited the same to a thousand pounds, he was pleased if it were not already filled your lordship with the opinion of the rest of the lords mentioned in the warrant might enlarge it to some reasonable increase as you should think meet. I moved his Majesty   5 thereupon that if it pleased him there might be a new warrant made without a limitation of a sum but left to such bills as by your initials should be signed and allowed. His Majesty seemed to like it well and if it please your lordship to think it a fit way it may be done ...

Calendar of State Papers Domestic, James I, vol. 37, p. 96, quoted in
G. P. Putnam, *The Court Masques of James I: Their Influence on Shakespeare and Public Theatres*, 1913, p. 201

5.6 Sir John Harington on the entertainment at Theobalds, 1606

One day a great feast was held; and, after dinner the representation of Solomon his Temple and the coming of the Queen of Sheba was made, or (as I may better say) was meant to have been made, before their Majesties, by Device of the Earl of Salisbury and others. But, alas! ... The Lady who did play the Queen's part, did carry most precious gifts to both their Majesties; but, forgetting the steps arising to the canopy,   5
overset her casket into his Danish Majesty's lap, and fell at his feet, though I rather think it was in his face. Much was the hurry and confusion. Cloths and napkins were at hand, to make all clean. His Majesty then got up, and would dance with the Queen of Sheba; but he fell down, and humbled himself before her, and was carried to an inner chamber and laid on a bed of state; which was not a little defiled with the   10
presents of the Queen, which had been bestowed on his garments; such as wine, cream, jelly, beverage, cake, spices, and other good matters ...

I have much marvelled at these strange pageantries, and they do bring to my remembrance what passed of this sort in our Queen's days; of which I was sometime an humble presenter and assistant: but I never did see such a lack of good order,   15
discretion, and sobriety as I have now done.

I have passed much time in seeing the royal sports of hunting and hawking, where the manners were such as made me devise the beasts were pursuing the sober creation, and not man in quest of exercise and food.

J. Nichols, *The Progresses of King James I*, vol. 2, 1828, p. 72

5.7 The splendour of the court

The splendour of the King, Queen, prince and princess with the rest of the royal issue, the concourse of strangers hither from foreign nations, the multitude of our own people from all parts of our three kingdoms gave a wonderful glory to the Court, at this time, the only theatre of Majesty; not any way inferior to the most magnificent in Christendom ...

William Sanderson, *A Compleat History of the Lives and Reigns of Mary Queen of Scots and of her Son and Successor, James*, 1656, p. 366

Questions

1   On what grounds does the draft letter from the Council in 1604 [5.4] urge James to think very carefully about the masque for Christmas 1604?
2   What light do **5.4** and **5.6** throw on the contrasting tones of the courts of Elizabeth I and James I?
3   How would James I and the author of **5.7** justify such expenses as are indicated by **5.5**?

By 1607, the halcyon days of March 1603 were well and truly over as far as money was concerned. In the following letter, James assumes the role of a financially sick man appealing to his doctor for help.

5.8 A letter from James I to the Council, October 1607

My Lords,

The only disease and consumption which I can ever apprehend as likeliest to endanger me is this eating canker of want, which being removed, I could think myself as happy in all other respects as any other king or monarch that ever was since the birth of Christ. In this disease I am the patient, and ye have promised to be the   5
physicians and to use the best cure upon me that your wits, faithfulness, and diligence can reach unto. As for my part, ye may assure yourselves that I shall facilitate your cure by all means possible for a poor patient, both by observing as strait a diet as ye can in honour and reason prescribe unto me, as also by using seasonably and in the right form such remedies and antidotes as ye are to apply   10
unto my disease.

The Letters of King James VI and I, ed. G. P. V. Akrigg, 1984, no. 136

Questions

1   James uses the doctor–patient model in this extract. Bearing in mind his attitude to doctors displayed in **1.13**, how convincing is his sincerity?
2   In view of the advice given in **5.4** and his behaviour in **5.5–5.7**, is James a financial no-hoper?

James frequently asserts the importance of safeguarding his 'honour' and his willingness to eliminate 'needless superfluities'. The following letter written in 1623 shows close regard for his 'honour' as represented by Prince Charles and George Villiers, Duke of Buckingham, at Madrid.

5.9 Letter from James I to Prince Charles and the Duke of Buckingham en route for Madrid, 1623

I send you also the jewels as I promised, some of mine and such of yours – I mean both of you – as are worthy the sending, ay, or my Baby's[1] presenting his mistress. I send him an old double cross of Lorrain ... a good looking glass with my picture in it, to be hung at her girdle ...

Ye shall present her with two fair diamonds, set like an anchor, and a fair pendent   5
diamond hanging in them. Ye shall give her a goodly rope of pearls, ye shall give a carquanet or collar, thirteen great ballas rubies, and thirteen knots or conques of pearls; and ye shall give her a head-dressing of two and twenty great pear pearls; and ye shall give her three goodly pear pendent diamonds, whereof the biggest to be worn at a needle on the midst of her forehead, and one in each ear.   10

And for my Baby's own wearing, ye shall have two good jewels of your own, your round broach of diamonds, and your triangle diamond with the great round pearl. And I send for your wearing The Three Brethren, that ye know full well, but newly set, and the Mirror of France, the fellow of the Portugal diamond, which I would wish you to wear alone in your hat, with a little black feather. Ye have also good   15
diamond buttons of your own, to be set to a doublet or jerkin ...

James R

[1] Baby = Prince Charles

Intimate Letters of England's Kings, ed. **Margaret Sanders**, 1959, p. 62

Questions

1   How would you argue that this letter, while demonstrating James's concern for his 'honour', was more likely to damage the image of monarchy if it became public knowledge?
2   What justification, if any, might be advanced for the extravagance of the 1623 visit to Madrid?

James's devotion to his 'honour' has been proved to be a constant theme in his attitude to his financial plight. His 'honour' required an increased revenue; his subjects hoped for a reduction in burdens as can be seen by the following petition at the beginning of the reign [5.10] and the report by the Venetian ambassador on Parliament's attitude to subsidies [5.11].

The grievances of the subject and Parliament

5.10 Part of The Poor Man's Petition to the king at Theobalds, 17 April 1603

Good King … A plague upon all covetous Treasurers! Good King, look to thy Takers and Officers of the House, and to their exceeding fees, that peele and powle[1] thy Princely allowance.

Good King, let us not be oppressed with so many impositions, powlings,[1] and payments.

[1] powle/powlings = tax

Nichols, *The Progresses of James I*, vol. 1, p. 127

5.11 Nicolo Molin, Venetian ambassador in England, to the doge and Senate, 9 November 1605

The principal business before Parliament is the granting of a subsidy,[1] which the King greatly desires, but it is generally supposed that he will meet with serious difficulties, and that it will be refused; for many members openly declare that as there is no war with Spain, no war in Holland, no army on the Scottish border – which they say cost the late Queen upwards of a million a year in gold – they cannot   5
understand why the King, who has the revenues of Scotland should want money. They add that the people are far more heavily burdened than under the late Queen, for the King stays so continually and so long in the country, where the peasants are obliged to furnish beasts and waggons for transporting the Court from place to place, and whenever he goes a-hunting the crops are mostly ruined. Further the Court   10
is far larger than in the late Queen's time, and the peasants are forced to supply provisions at low prices, which is an intolerable burden. The late Queen insisted that her officers should take care not to requisition more than was necessary, but now no attention is paid to this, and the officers exact twice as much as is required and sell the surplus at high prices, thus enriching themselves and ruining the peasants. All   15
this is put about by those who have little wish to satisfy the King; and the issue is extremely doubtful.

[1] subsidy = a tax levied by Parliament

Calendar of State Papers Venetian, vol. 10, p. 285

Questions

1 Compare and contrast **5.10** and **5.11** in how they apportion the blame for burdens.
2 What justification was there for expecting a reduction in financial burdens under a new dynasty?

3   What were the implications for James I of the comparison with Elizabeth
in **5.11**, **5.4** and **5.6**?

James's First Parliament was quick to raise the grievances of fiscal feudalism.
Devices such as wardship and purveyance were deeply unpopular, as indicated
by **5.12** and **5.13**. Robert Cecil favoured ending wardship but met with such
vested interest from office holders that he was forced to abandon his early
scheme and concentrate on boosting the income from this source. It was
almost trebled by the end of James's reign. He also had sympathy with the
victims of purveyance, but necessity required additional court expenses, and
alternative means of providing for the court in sufficient profusion were not
forthcoming.

5.12 The Lower House on wardship, 1604

We cannot forget how your Majesty ... advised us, for unjust burdens, to proceed
against them by bill; but for such as were just, to come to yourself by way of petition,
with tender of such ... composition in profit as for the supporting of your royal
estate was requisite. According to which, we prepared a petition for leave to treat
with your highness touching a perpetual composition to be raised by yearly revenue,   5
out of the lands of your subjects, for Wardships and other burdens, depending on
them ... Wherein we first considered that this prerogative of the Crown, which we
desired to compound for, was a matter of mere profit and not of any princely dignity
...

Secondly, we considered the great grievance and damage to the subject by the decay
of many houses and the mischief of many forced and ill-suited marriages, and lastly   10
the great contempt and reproach of our nation in all foreign countries, by the small
commodity now raised to the Crown in respect of that which, with thankfulness for
the restitution of this original right in disposing of our children, we would be glad to
assure unto your Majesty.

Thirdly, we considered that [as] the original of these Wardships was serving of the   15
King in his wars against Scotland (which cause we hope now to be at an everlasting
end), your Majesty might be pleased to accept an offer of our perpetual and certain
revenue not only proportionable to the utmost benefit that any of your progenitors
ever reaped thereby, but also with such an overplus and large addition, as in great
part to supply your Majesty's other occasions, that our ease might breed your plenty.

Historical Manuscripts Commission, *Calendar of the Manuscripts of the*
Most Honourable The Marquess of Salisbury, **p. 141**

5.13 Sir Francis Bacon's speech on purveyance to the king at Whitehall, 16 June 1604

... There was no grievance in his kingdom so general, so continual, so sensible,[1] and so bitter to the common subject, as that which he was then speaking of [Purveyance]; that they do not pretend to derogate from his prerogative, nor to question any of his regalities or rights; they only seek a reformation of abuses and restoration of the laws to which they were born ... The Purveyors take in kind what they ought not to take; 5 they take in quantity a far greater proportion than cometh to the King's use; and they take in an unlawful manner ... There is no pound of profit to him but begetteth three pound damages on the subject; by abuse they take at an enforced price ... This abuse of Purveyance, if it be not the most heinous abuse, yet it is the most common and general abuse of all others in the kingdom.

[1] sensible = keenly felt

Nichols, *The Progresses of James I*, vol. 1, p. xii

Questions

1 Why were wardship and purveyance such contentious issues?
2 How does **5.12** use the argument of 'honour' against the interests of the king in 1604?
3 What were the advantages and disadvantages to the Crown from the continuation of wardship and purveyance?
4 What problems might be faced by James I if he accepted composition (a monetary settlement) for wardship and purveyance?

These feudal devices were to fester until the Long Parliament of Charles I abolished them. They were symptomatic of deficiencies which required the sort of radical treatment that had been promised in the abortive Great Contract of 1610. James's revenue was heavily dependent on income from Crown lands and customs. Remedies to improve both were pressed in the early years of the reign. In the long run they met with little success as the average yearly income from Crown lands dropped from £128,257 in 1603 to £95,430 in 1621.

The most profitable and one of the most hated money-raising schemes was the use of impositions. Before 1608 they yielded little; thereafter they promised a much needed elastic source of revenue. The justification for them was provided by the case against John Bate, a merchant importing currants from the Levant, who had refused to pay impositions on the grounds that they were over and above the customs schedules agreed by Parliament and not, therefore, approved by Parliament. The case was heard in the Court of the Exchequer Chamber.

5.14 Bate's case, 1606

Baron Clarke's Judgment

... [It] seemeth to me strange that any subjects would contend with the King in this high point of prerogative ... And as it is not a kingdom without subjects and government, so he is not a King without revenues ... and he who rendeth that from the King pulleth also his crown from his head, for it cannot be separated from the Crown. And such great prerogatives of the Crown, without which it cannot be, ought 5 not to be disputed; and in these cases of prerogative the judgment shall not be according to the rules of the Common Law, but according to the precedents of this Court wherein these matters are disputable and determinable ...

Chief Baron Fleming's Judgment

... The King's power is double, ordinary and absolute ... All customs, be they old or new, are no other but the effects and issues of trades and commerce with foreign 10 nations; but all commerce and affairs with foreigners, all wars and peace, all acceptance and admitting for current, foreign coin, all parties and treaties whatsoever, are made by the absolute power of the King ... No exportation or importation can be but at the King's ports. They are the gates of the King, and he hath absolute power by them to include or exclude whom he shall please ... It is 15 reasonable that the King should have as much power over foreigners and their goods as over his own subjects; and if the King cannot impose upon foreign commodities a custom as well as foreigners may upon their own commodities and upon the commodities of this land when they come to them, then foreign States shall be enriched and the King impoverished ...

J. R. Tanner, *Constitutional Documents of the Reign of James I, 1603–1625,* 1961, pp. 338–40

5.15 A letter from John Chamberlain to Sir Ralph Winwood, London, 24 May 1610

Touching parliament matters I know not what to write, seeing they have sit now fourteen weeks to so little purpose. Of late there has been some tempests raised about their meddling with impositions, which by a message from the King they were forbidden to deal in, but because the message came not *modo et forma,*[1] nor immediately (as they took it) from the King they did in a sort refuse to take notice of 5 it. Whereupon grew more messages and much contestation, but in the end they ... with a moderate answer pacified his Majesty so that ... he made another speech to both houses, but so little to their satisfaction, that I hear it bred generally much discomfort; to see our monarchical power and regal prerogative strained so high and made so transcendent every way, that if the practice should follow the positions, we 10 are not like to leave our successors that freedom we received from our forefathers, nor make account of any thing we have longer than they list that govern …

¹ *modo et forma* = in the appropriate form

The Letters of John Chamberlain, ed. N. E. Clure, 1939, vol. 1, p. 300

5.16 The debate on impositions, 23 June to 3 July 1610

Mr Hakewill's Argument

Mr Speaker, The question now in debate amongst us is, whether his Majesty may by his prerogative royal, without assent of Parliament, at his own will and pleasure, lay a new charge or imposition upon merchandises to be brought out of this kingdom of England, and enforce merchants to pay the same? …

… I … maintain … this position: That the Common Law of England giveth to the   5
King … no perpetual revenue or matter of profit out of the interest or property of the subject but it either limiteth a certainty therein at the first, or otherwise hath so provided that if it be uncertain in itself it is reducable to a certainty only by a legal course, that is to say, either by Parliament, by judges, or jury; and not by the King's own absolute will and pleasure …   10

'The ports and haven towns of England are', say they, 'the King's, and in regard thereof he may open and shut them upon what conditions he pleaseth.' I answer, That the position that all the ports are the King's is not generally true; for subjects may also be owners of ports … But admitting the truth of the position, yet is the consequence as weak and dangerous as of any of the rest of their arguments. For are   15
not all the gates of cities and towns, and all the streets and highways in England the King's, and as much subject to be open and shut at his pleasure as the ports are?

Another of their arguments is this. That the King is bound to protect merchants from spoil by the enemy; he ought to fortify the havens … he ought … to send ambassadors to foreign princes to negotiate for them … It is reason therefore that his   20
expense be defrayed out of the profit made by merchants, and consequently that he may impose upon merchandise a moderate charge thereby to repay himself … But it is no good consequence that therefore he may take what he list, no more than he may at his pleasure increase that old revenue which the law giveth him for protecting of subjects in their suits or for protecting wards, etc.   25

If … the levying of impositions be indeed the only means that is left to redress the inconvenience, why should not that be done by Act of Parliament …?

So I conclude that impositions, neither in time of war … much less in time of peace, neither upon foreign or inland commodities of whatsoever nature … neither upon merchants strangers nor denizens, may be laid by the King's absolute power without   30
assent of Parliament, be it for never so short a time, much less to endure for ever, as ours.

Tanner, *Constitutional Documents of the Reign of James I*, pp. 247ff.

Questions

1 Why did impositions generate such deep feelings in the 1610 session of Parliament?
2 Analyse the arguments of Clarke and Fleming in **5.14**.
3 In what ways was the royal prerogative challenged by the debates on impositions in 1610 [**5.15, 5.16**]?
4 How effectively were the arguments of the Exchequer barons countered by Hakewill in 1610?
5 How does Chamberlain suggest that there were other important issues than the royal prerogative at stake in attitudes to impositions [**5.15**]?

The efforts of James's ministers to create a solvent monarchy

Against such articulate pressing of grievances stood the Lord Treasurer and Chancellor of the Exchequer. Theirs was indeed a thankless task. It is easy to suggest that all Jacobean ministers with the exception of Cecil and Cranfield were lightweights. The following exchange of letters between Sir Julius Caesar and the Earl of Dorset illustrates their very considerable difficulties.

5.17 Letter from the Earl of Dorset to Sir Julius Caesar, 31 May 1607

I have just signed your two orders, and do greatly thank you for delivering my most humble thanks to his Majesty. As for clamours for money when there is no means to pay, that is new to you, but not to me. I know not, nor no man earthly knows, any other remedy but to answer them that they must tarry 'til it come in ... As for my coming to London, I know not a halfpenny of help that I can give you thereby, if I were fit, or able; and I thank humbly his Majesty he hath given me credit to seek to recover my health, which I desire to do for his service.   5
T. Dorset

Edmund Lodge, *The Life of Julius Caesar*, 1827, pp. 25–26

5.18 Letter from the Earl of Dorset to Sir Julius Caesar, not dated but endorsed by Caesar on 9 June 1607

Now, Mr Chancellor, touching your lamentation of the clamours and suits that are daily made to you for money ... I can say but this; that true fortitude is never daunted, and truth ought never to be either afraid or ashamed. You may truly answer them that the King's debts, his subsidies, his rents, his revenues, notwithstanding all the means of levying of them that possibly may be devised, are not paid, but   5
piecemeal come in, with great difficulty; and how can the King's Majesty pay what he owes when that which is owing to him is unpaid? Besides, his Majesty hath brought with him an increase of a most comfortable charge; as of a Queen ... a

Prince; and other his most royal progeny: These are comfortable charges, and all good subjects must help willingly to bear the burden thereof – That the King of   10
Spain himself, that hath so many Indian gold and silver mines to help him, doth yet leave his debts many times unpaid – That the King's Majesty, and his Council, do not neglect to devise all possible means and ways to bring in moneys – That as the King's revenues do come in, so they shall have part and part among them; for one must not have all, and the rest nothing. These, and such like, are true answers, and   15
ought, and must, satisfy ... Now, Mr Chancellor, if three weeks be so grievous unto you, what will you think of my grief that in this kind have endured the grief of three years? ...

Lodge, *The Life of Julius Caesar*, p. 26

Questions

1   What offices were held by the Earl of Dorset and Sir Julius Caesar?
2   Compare and contrast the attitudes of Dorset and Caesar to their work.
3   How does Dorset account for the king's financial problems?
4   What 'clamours and suits' [5.18, line 1] are likely to have been made to Caesar for money?
5   In what ways and with what success had James I tried to remedy his financial situation by 1607?

Robert Cecil was indeed of sterner stuff. He was James's secretary, Master of the Wards and, after 1608, Lord Treasurer. That was the year in which he began the building of the present Hatfield House, which he acquired by exchanging his residence at Theobalds with the king. He tried very hard to rescue James from the pitfalls of raising loans at 10 per cent, selling Crown land and exploiting the feudal fiscal devices. He found blame rather than cooperation from the king whom he served, and unpopularity from those within and without the Parliament whose vested interests he threatened. His integrity and commitment is shown by the realistic nature of the advice he gives James and the hard line he takes with the king [5.19]. It is followed by bleak advice from the Council whose tone shows a situation of deep crisis [5.20].

5.19   Robert Cecil advises frugality

... For certainly Sir, though the liberality and goodness that lieth in you are virtues, worthy of you as you are a great king, yet they are somewhat improper for this kingdom, which being compared with other monarchies may certainly be counted potent, but not opulent ...

I am of opinion … that it is not possible for a king of England, much less of Great   5
Britain … to be rich or safe, but by frugality …

**'A collection of several speeches and treatises of the late Lord Treasurer
Cecil, and of several observations of the Lords of the Council given to King
James concerning his estate and revenue in the years 1608, 1609 and 1610',
ed. Pauline Croft, *The Camden Miscellany*, vol. 29, 1987, pp. 273–319**

5.20 Robert Cecil advises James on his approach to Parliament

For surely Sir, although it be true that liberality be one of the excellentest virtues in a
king, yet we could wish your Majesty to be better persuaded that the exercise of that
virtue in this estate as it now standeth may generate many errors, especially if in the
distribution there be not some care and caution observed …

… Having sifted and searched every corner of invention find no means to supply   5
your growing and great necessities otherwise than by parliament …

The first, that it will be much for your Majesty's advantage, to forbear all
extraordinary gifts to private men at this time that you are to demand help and
supply for yourself and your posterity.

Secondly, that neither for yourself nor any other you insist too much upon your   10
prerogative, because the courses to be held in parliament, and the use of that power
(as it reacheth at the money and means of your people) coming now both together,
make worse passage to both. Instead of which we would rather wish that your
majesty would be pleased to value your grace and bounty to your parliament, with
dispensing with some of that monarchical power which is inherent in your royal   15
person …

The third consideration is in the time of the sitting, to make your wants so clear and
visible as may be believed and the cause thereof not altogether scandalized. All which
must be handled with such discretion as the lower house may not be made the king's
auditors, nor censurers of their sovereign's actions.

Croft, *The Camden Miscellany*, vol. 29, pp. 300ff.

Questions

1 Document **5.19** seems to lay the blame for James's financial situation on
   the king himself. How justified is this?
2 What advice is offered in **5.19** and **5.20** for remedying the financial
   situation?
3 What form would the parliamentary solution take in 1610?
4 How might James achieve cooperation with, rather than control by,
   Parliament in financial affairs?

5.21 Sir Julius Caesar on the Great Contract, 1610[1]

17th August, 1610. Q. Whether that this contract between the King and the two Houses of Parliament be profitable for the King or no?

A. It appeareth that the King shall gain thereby a yearly addition to his other revenue	£200,000	
C (Caesar?) True, did it not also appear that this bargain taketh yearly from the King, which before he held uncontrollably by his just prerogative, the wards and tenures, with their incidents … etc., worth yearly to the King	£44,000	5
The purveyances of the King's house and stable …	£50,000	10
Assarts,[2] defective titles, informations upon penal statutes, and such other lawful advantages and prerogatives quitted[3] and released in the several retributions[4] yielded unto on his Majesty's behalf	£21,000	
All which amount unto	£115,000	15
There will remain to the King towards the increase of his yearly revenue but	£85,000	

But with the loss of such power and command over his subjects in so high points of prerogative as never yet could be obtained from any of his progenitors, Kings or Queens of this realm.

Now the question will be, whether the King may not, without wronging the subjects, raise that £85,000 by improvement of those things so parted with by this bargain? And questionless it seemeth that he may.

20

[1] This is a fragment of an imaginary conversation held by Caesar on the Great Contract. As Chancellor of the Exchequer Caesar wished to see that the king did not lose out when feudal incidents were surrendered for an annual £200,000.
[2] assarts = conversion of land to arable
[3] quitted = cancelled
[4] retributions = repayments

Tanner, *Constitutional Documents of the Reign of James I*, p. 348

Questions

1   What was Julius Caesar's advice to the king on the Great Contract?
2   How did he reach his conclusion?
3   What factors might limit the elasticity of the feudal incidents?
4   Considering the broad perspective of the problem, how far would you support Caesar's advice?

5.22 A speech by the Lord Treasurer during the 1610 session of Parliament

I [Cecil] will not say his case [James I's] is so miserable and desperate that without the parliament relieve he cannot subsist ... But this I'll say, if the parliament relieve him not, you leave him in great extremity, and the consequence is dangerous both to the King and the people ...

The King's debts multiply; his expenses have been more than was expected at the   5
last session ...

... This contract is a child born after much difficulty, a king full of apprehension, a lower House full of doubt, was at last lapped up and swaddled. But do not I know that the midwife or nurse may so swaddle or lay up the child as 'tis opened they find a lame child?[1] It may be laid up so loosely as the child may be disjointed, it may be   10
lapped up so hard as it will be lame. Cram him not; 'twill choke him. If you keep him too long without meat he will perish ...

[1] Cecil probably has in mind the infirmity suffered by himself and his daughter.

Proceedings in Parliament 1610, ed. E. R. Foster, vol. 2, 1966, pp. 297ff.

Questions

1   What were the main terms of the Great Contract?
2   Why and with what consequences was Parliament reluctant to conclude the Contract?
3   Examine the attitude of James I to the Great Contract in **5.23**. What part did he play in the failure of the Great Contract?
4   What evidence is there that James was following the advice of Julius Caesar given in **5.21** rather than that of his Lord Treasurer given in **5.20**?

5.23 A letter from James I to a committee of the House of Lords concerning the Great Contract, March? 1610

My Lords,

According to my promise unto you yesternight, I do by these presents let you know that I crave seven score thousand pounds by year in retribution of such things as I am to bargain for with the parliament at this time. I mean this sum to be of clear addition to that which formerly I did spend by the natures of those things that are now to be   5
bargained for. And with this my demand ye are now to acquaint the committees of the lower house.

James R

Akrigg, *Letters*, no. 148

After the failure of the Great Contract, Cecil became ill. Before his death from stomach cancer in 1612 he had thought up the scheme of selling the title of baronet as a source of income for the Crown. The aim was to raise money for the settlement of Ireland; it generated £90,000 during the period 1611–14. This became one of a series of financial expedients in the post-Cecil era, a period which began with the additional burdens of the funeral of Prince Henry and the expensive wedding celebrations of Princess Elizabeth and the Elector Frederick in 1613.

5.24 The king's bounty, 1614

The King's bounty has stretched beyond the liberty of his treasure, which he timely took up, and was free in rewarding merit by Honour of Knighthood, upon such whose estates were not answerable in value to other gentry, before whom they were to take place of precedency, and therefore it was designed (twelve months since) by the late Treasurer Salisbury, to create a degree of knight baronets to proceed all knight   5
bachelors ... ninety persons in all of good birth and estates, and each of them (except 22) were then knight bachelors, and was done saith a good author to my knowledge, for I copied the list of them before it was presented to Salisbury ...

And herein other Princes exceed in Example, and were never quarrelled at by any, as in Germany, Spain, France, Italy, Venice; and must it now be a crime in this king, in   10
the settlement of his inheritance here, to take leave to advance the creation of one single order?

The Annals of King James and King Charles I, **printed by Thomas Braddyl for R. Clavel, 1681**

Questions

1   Why did Salisbury suggest the scheme of selling the title of baronet and what were its implications for the peerage?
2   How convincingly are possible objections to the scheme dismissed in 5.24?

After the death of Cecil, James resorted to piecemeal attempts to solve his problems. He granted the fateful monopoly to Alderman Cockayne in 1614, sold the Cautionary Towns (Flushing, Brille and Rammekens) to the Dutch – towns which had been given to England by the Dutch in the reign of Elizabeth I as security for Dutch debts to England – borrowed money and sold Crown lands. No radical attempt to solve the financial situation was made after the Great Contract. The most able of his later advisers was Lionel Cranfield, later Earl of Middlesex, an able man from a merchant background with a very efficient civil servant mind; even he could do no more than urge retrenchment from 1618 until his fall from power in 1624.

5.25 Letter from the Reverend Thomas Lorkin to Sir Thomas Puckering, 16 June 1618

Sir Lionel Cranfield hath troubled much the household officers at court, by laying down a project to the King of saving him £12,000 a year in ordinary expense, and yet no man abridged of his allowance, which is, with this condition, imposed upon the said officers that either they must make it good, or resign up their places unto him.

T. Birch, *Court and Times of James I*, 1973 reprint of the 1849 edition, vol. 2, p. 75

5.26 Lorkin to Puckering, Greenwich, 30 June 1618

There are many busy here how to bring within compass the King's ordinary expense. Yesterday they cut off four of the ships upon the narrow seas; that whereas heretofore eight attended that service – now the moiety must serve the turn. They are in hand, likewise, to bring a reformation into the stables; and every way is thought upon how to set the King straight, but the right.

Birch, *Court and Times of James I*, vol. 2, p. 126

Questions

1   Why were the attempts of Cranfield likely to be unpopular?
2   In what other ways and with what success did Cranfield try to improve the royal finances?

If James had been seriously committed to retrenchment, the court masques would have been reduced in scale. There is no evidence of such economy. In fact, the Whitehall fire of January 1619 enabled the building of the Inigo Jones masterpiece that became a magnificent temple to Stuart aspirations. The new Banqueting House was completed by 1622 during a period in which James was heavily committed to building. It must be remembered that he was the patron of the finest Palladian architecture in England. The positive side to his resistance to frugality can be measured in the Banqueting House, the Chapel Royal and the Queen's House at Greenwich, to mention only the most famous royal commissions to Inigo Jones. As the Banqueting House was rising, Bacon and Cranfield struggled with issues of monopolies and war finance. Cranfield had no desire to see the proliferation of monopolies; he regarded them as restrictive of trade. The issue of monopolies with its attendant corruption, together with war finance, restricted Cranfield's achievements at the end of the reign. Sir Giles Mompesson and Lord Chancellor Bacon fell victim to impeachment as the House attacked monopolists and those who had been referees for patents.

Monopolies and financial crisis, 1620–25

5.27 Letter to the Marquis of Buckingham, 29 November 1620

My very good Lord,

Your Lordship may find that in the number of patents which we have represented to his Majesty as like to be stirred in by the Lower House of Parliament, we have set down three which may concern some of your Lordship's special friends, which I account as mine own friends; and so showed myself when they were in suit. The one, that to Sir G Mompesson, touching the inns; the second to Mr Christopher Villiers and Mr Maule, touching the recognizances from ale-houses: the third, to Mr Lieutenant of the Tower, touching the cask ...

Letters and Life of Francis Bacon, ed. James Spedding, 1874, vol. 7, p. 148

5.28 The revival of impeachment: Sir Giles Mompesson

5.28(a) A Commons' Committee, 28 February 1621

Sir Edward Coke: The court of Parliament a Court of Counsel and a Court of Pleas ... Complaints and examinations of grievances have been ancient in the House of Commons, the matter of fact tried there; they have often resorted to the Lords for judicature ... Never any that was found guilty hath been able to bear out the storm of the Commons forces.

5.28(b) Later in the House

Sir Edward Coke made report from the committee for the search of precedents ... Therefore we are resolved according to former precedents to address ourselves to the Lords, for so it was in Henry the Sixth's time ...

5.28(c) Proceedings in the Lords

12 March: The Lord Chancellor ... reported what passed at the conference of both Houses, the inducement of which conference was to clear the King's honour touching grants to Sir Giles Mompesson ...

26 March, The King's Speech: ... I intend not to derogate or infringe any of the liberties or privileges of this House, but rather to fortify and strengthen them ... I know ye will do nothing but what the like hath been done before ... For I acknowledge this to be the Supreme Court of Justice, wherein I am ever present by representation ...

26 March, afternoon: Message sent to the lower House ... that if the Commons with
their Speaker, will according to the ancient custom of Parliament come to demand of   10
the Lords that judgment be given against Sir Giles Mompesson for the heinous
offences by him committed, they shall be heard ...

[Their] Lordships received divers instructions from [the Commons], and thereupon,
proceeding by examinations of divers witnesses upon oath, they find Sir Giles
Mompesson, and divers others, guilty of many heinous crimes against the   15
Commonwealth ...

And so [the Lord Chief Justice, in the absence of the Lord Chancellor] pronounced
the judgment of the Lords against Sir Giles Mompesson.

5.28(a) and (b)*Commons Debates 1621*, ed. W. Notestein, F. H. Relf and
H. Simpson, 1935, vol. 4, 115–16 and 148–49. 5.28(c) *Lords Journal*, vol. 3,
pp. 33–72. All quoted in J. P. Kenyon, *The Stuart Constitution*, **1966, pp. 98–100**

Questions

1   Why had monopolies become such an issue in the 1621 Parliament?
2   How were Bacon and Villiers threatened by the attack on monopolists?
3   What was the significance of the revival of impeachment in 1621? What
    was an impeachment?
4   What part was played by finance in the disagreements between king and
    Parliament in 1621?

5.29 Financial issues in 1621: Girolamo Lando, Venetian ambassador in England, to the doge and Senate, 18 June 1621

They have not actually granted the king one penny more than the two subsidies,
previously given to help him, so that he may recall them and because they are most
determined not to give him any more until he has actually unsheathed the sword.

Cal State Papers Venetian, vol. 17, p. 67

Question

1   The Venetian ambassador suggests that Parliament was using the
    financial weapon against the king in 1621 to manipulate foreign policy.
    How far do you agree with this verdict? With what success was this
    weapon used?

5.30 Lionel Cranfield's notes for a speech to Parliament, November 1621

Whether ever the people of England lived eighteen years together in such peace and
plenty and with so little charge to their King as they have done since his Majesty's
reign.

The staple commodities of the kingdom, viz. wool, corn, yea, and even of land itself
hath so continued all his Highness's reign until this last two years.   5

The people notwithstanding all this improvement to their estates never since the
Conquest gave so little to their King in eighteen years as they have done to his
Majesty.

But that which his Majesty is most sensible of, these benefits of his Highness's reign
are so far from being thankfully acknowledged as some make use of them to his   10
prejudice. For wool and corn by reason of plenty and and some foreign accidents
being within these two years fallen in price, and trade by like foreign occasions of late
being somewhat in decline and yet all of them in more flourishing estate than when
his Majesty came to the Crown, the murmuring and grudging of some ill affected
against the present government is such as would grieve any honest man to hear.   15

The general cry is of the poverty of the people. If eighteen years with a flourishing
trade and one third part improvement of all the staple commodities of the kingdom
for so long time together will not make the people rich, they have strangely abused
God's blessing under his Majesty's government …

O happy exchange! And which may not be forgotten that land which was not worth   20
£400 when his Majesty came to the Crown is now worth £4,000 so that it may be
truly said the land in Ireland is improved not one in ten, but ten in one and the land
in England one third since his Majesty's reign.

Notestein, Relf and Simpson, *The Commons Debates,* **vol. 7, pp. 617–19**

Questions

1   On what grounds and with what success did Cranfield argue that the
     criticisms and complaints of 'the poverty of the people' **[5.30, line 16]**
     were not justified?
2   Why did such an appeal fail to elicit generous subsidies from the 1621
     Parliament?

5.31 Financial incapacity: Girolamo Lando, Venetian ambassador in England, to the doge and Senate, 6 January 1622

The King submitted to the Council the proposal already reported to collect a force of
14,000 foot and 4,000 horse, so that it might decide how to lay the matter before
parliament to obtain the money to support it. But the councillors, thinking it
impossible to induce them to incur such an expense, which would certainly arouse
much ill-feeling in the kingdom … decided upon a smaller force of 8,000 foot and   5
1,500 horse. This has occasioned a wide-spread announcement of such a levy. But the
assembly being dispersed … everything remains immature and nothing is being
done. And there is no way of doing anything without money, the King having none
and can have none unless he has recourse to his friends. Even if it were done it would

prove inadequate to the necessities ... There is some fear that he may decide to   10
impose taxes on his own responsibility to obtain money, as every day it is suggested
to him that he should make his subjects absolutely obedient to him, as the King of
Spain does; which would be a great and perilous innovation.

Rumours circulate that the Spaniards will supply the King's need of money by the
dowry, though it is perfectly evident that they would not wish to supply any to enable   15
him to make war in the Palatinate.

Cal State Papers Venetian, vol. 17, p. 198

In a number of ways, the Palatinate crisis proved a catalyst. The financial
implications of the commitment to restore the hereditary lands of the Elector
Palatine were great. For extraordinary revenue for a war, Parliament
demanded consultation on policy, leading to the clash between parliamentary
privilege and the royal prerogative in the 1621 Parliament.

The failure of the Spanish marriage scheme required financial cooperation
with Parliament in the form of a Subsidy Act. Supplies voted to the king were
specifically tied to the war effort and account had to be given of how the
money was spent. The last Parliament saw the sacrifice of Cranfield, by now
an opponent of his erstwhile patron, Buckingham, and a resolute opponent of
war, which he saw as the harbinger of financial disaster. By 1625 peace had
failed, retrenchment had been only half-hearted, and attempts at reform had
revealed the power of vested interest and the fear of change. James was to
some extent a victim of circumstances and vested interests; his Treasurers
battled unsuccessfully with those forces, with vociferous Parliaments and with
royal inertia.

5.32 The Subsidy Act of 1624

I ... And therefore we do humbly beseech your Majesty that it may be declared and
enacted, and be it declared by the authority of this present Parliament, that the two
treaties (with Spain) are by your majesty utterly dissolved; And for the maintenance
of the war which may come thereupon, and for the causes aforesaid, be it enacted
that three whole Fifteenths and Tenths shall be paid, taken, and levied of the   5
moveable goods, chattels, and other things usual to such Fifteenths and Tenths ...

XXXIX And be it further enacted, That as well the said Treasurers as the said
persons appointed for the Council of War as aforesaid, and all other persons who
shall be trusted with the receiving, issuing, bestowing, and employing of these
moneys or any part thereof ... shall be answerable and accountable for their doings   10
or proceedings herein to the Commons in Parliament ...

Tanner, *Constitutional Documents*, **pp. 376ff.**

Questions

1 What financial options remained available to the king at the end of his Third Parliament? Examine the consequences of these options.
2 In what ways does the Subsidy Act reflect parliamentary initiative in financial affairs by 1624?
3 Discuss the view that the key to understanding James I's failure in money matters is to be found in his insistence upon the royal prerogative. Given the historical circumstances, was any lasting solution possible?
4 How far would you agree that money was the root of all evil between James I and his Parliaments?

Recommended reading

R. Ashton, *The Crown and the Money Market, 1603–1640*, 1960

T. Cogswell, 'A low road to extinction? Supply and redress of grievances in the Parliaments of the 1620s', *Historical Journal*, vol. 33, 1990

P. Croft, 'Free trade and the House of Commons, 1605–1606', *Economic History Review*, 2nd series, vol. 28, 1975

P. Croft, 'Wardship in the Parliament of 1604', *Parliamentary History*, vol. 2, 1983

P. Croft, 'Parliament, purveyance and the City of London, 1589–1608', *Parliamentary History*, vol. 4, 1985

P. Croft, 'Fresh light on Bate's case', *Historical Journal*, vol. 30, 1987

P. Croft (ed.), 'A collection of several speeches and treatises of the late Lord Treasurer Cecil, and of several observations of the Lords of the Council given to King James concerning his estates and revenue in the years 1608, 1609 and 1610', *The Camden Miscellany*, vol. 29, 1987, pp. 273–319

P. Croft, '"The reputation of Robert Cecil: libels, political opinion and popular awareness in the early seventeenth century', *Transactions of the Royal Historical Society*, 6th series, vol. 1, 1991

G. L. Harriss, 'Medieval doctrines in the debates on supply, 1610–1629', *Faction and Parliament*, ed. K. Sharpe, 1978

M. Prestwich, *Cranfield: Politics and Profits under the Early Stuarts*, 1966

A.G. R. Smith, 'Crown, Parliament and finance: The Great Contract of 1610', in *The English Commonwealth*, ed. P. Clark, A. G. R. Smith and N. Tyacke, 1979

D. Thomas, 'Financial and administrative developments', in *The English Civil War*, ed. H. Tomlinson, 1983

6 'Rex Pacificus'
The foreign policy of James I

Time chart	
1604	Treaty of London ended the war with Spain
1609	Truce of Antwerp (Twelve Years' Truce) between Spain and the Dutch Fishing disputes with the Dutch
1610	The Cleves–Julich crisis Assassination of Henry IV of France
1613	Whaling disputes with the Dutch off the coast of Greenland Marriage of the Princess Elizabeth to the Elector Palatine Arrival of Sarmiento (later Count Gondomar) as the Spanish ambassador to England
1614	Treaty of Xanten resolving the Cleves–Julich crisis The Cockayne Project provoked an adverse reaction from the Dutch
1618	Outbreak of the Thirty Years War in Bohemia
1619	Frederick of the Palatinate accepted the crown of Bohemia
1620	Defeat of Frederick at the Battle of the White Mountain Invasion of the Upper Palatinate by Maximilian of Bavaria on behalf of the Emperor
1621	End of the Truce of Antwerp
1622	Occupation of the Lower Palatinate by Spain
1623	Massacre of English merchants on Amboyna Mission of Prince Charles and Buckingham to Madrid
1624	War with Spain French marriage treaty Mansfeld's expedition to relieve the Palatinate

James I's personal motto, Beati Pacifici (Blessed are the Peacemakers), and his wish to be Rex Pacificus (the King of Peace), reflect more than impotent idealism derived from an aversion to violence and the choice of Solomon as role model. He saw foreign policy as a key area of royal prerogative, was aware of the financial consequences of European commitment, and genuinely sought peace and stability in Europe through diplomacy and dynastic marriages.

Interpretations of his foreign policy have been revised by the research of recent historians. The influence of Gondomar has been appraised by Charles Carter, that of Buckingham by Roger Lockyer, and Conrad Russell's analysis of early Stuart Parliaments has provoked Tim Cogswell's stimulating study of the war Parliaments of 1621 and 1624.

The foreign policy landmarks are dominated by Spain: the Treaty of London with Spain (1604); the Truce of Antwerp (1609), halting hostilities between the Dutch and the Spanish for twelve years; the attempted solutions to the Palatinate crisis that dominated foreign policy after 1618. The failure of the Spanish marriage scheme returned policy to that of hostility to Spain and a guarded friendship towards the Dutch.

Spain was seen as the 'natural enemy' at the beginning of the seventeenth century, an enemy aiming at 'universal monarchy' at the expense of everything dear to the English: religion, trade and nationality. Spain was the agent of the Counter Reformation, the champion of English Catholics, undermining the State from within and blocking enterprise in the New World. By contrast, the Protestant Dutch, fighting for their independence from Spain, appeared as a natural ally until their commercial expansion threatened English interests.

By 1603 the old order was changing: the deaths of Philip II of Spain in 1598 and Elizabeth of England in 1603 removed the need for war. James sought the loyalty of English Roman Catholics and a period of peace in which to consolidate his accession and control over the three kingdoms (Scotland, England and Wales, and Ireland); above all he had to avoid the financial drain and parliamentary wrangling that accompanied war.

Peace with Spain

6.1 Simon Contarini, Venetian ambassador in Spain, to the doge and Senate, 24 May 1603

The King [Philip III of Spain] is entirely occupied about the question of a peace with England, and has abandoned for the present all other business. They are waiting to see what kind of answer the King of England will return to an ambassador ... His Majesty has given orders to all his ships that if they fall in with Englishmen they are

not to molest them; and also that if any English ships arrive in Spanish harbours   5
with passports signed by the King of England ... they are to be well received. I am
informed that the King of England is also much inclined to peace, and that he has
prevented certain privateers, fitted out to harass Spaniards, from sailing ... Here they
show great relief at the death of the Queen of England [Elizabeth I], and they declare
that affairs in Flanders are already looking more favourable for the King [Philip III]   10
than they were some months ago ... And in very truth, owing to the Queen's death, a
few days have sufficed to change the aspect of matters from one of despair to one of
hope.

Calendar of State Papers Venetian, vol. 10, p. 37

6.2 Giovanni Carlo Scaramelli, Venetian ambassador in England, to the doge and Senate, 12 June 1603

As the King [James I] is by nature of a mild disposition, and has never really been
happy in Scotland ... so he desires to have no bother with other people's affairs and
little with his own; he would like to dedicate himself to his books and to the chase,
and to encourage the opinion that he is the real arbiter of peace. He has a suspicion
in his mind because he has heard that the Pope has occasionally discussed the   5
possibility of uniting France and Spain against England as well as against the Turks,
and for this reason he is resolved, if possible, to stand well with all Catholic Princes
and with Your Serenity [the Doge] in particular. He will draw close to the strongest
of them, the King of Spain, and will seek to gratify the Emperor, while he is bound
to the Protestant Princes by his religion; and in this way he calculates that he can   10
secure the friendship of France and even the alliance of France and the respect of the
whole world. From these calculations, made in Scotland and carried with him in
England, the English find it difficult to move his Majesty.

Cal State Papers Venetian, vol. 10, p. 48

Questions

1 Explain why you would handle information from the documents above
   with caution. What are the advantages and disadvantages of this genre of
   source?

2 How convincing do you find Scaramelli's explanation of James's motives
   for peace with Spain? What other explanations may be offered for his
   policy?

3 In what way is 'Flanders' relevant to Anglo-Spanish relations [6.1, line
   10]?

4 What evidence is there in the extracts that the desire for peace between
   England and Spain was mutual?

5 The author of 6.2 implies that the English had reservations about the

king's policies. For what reasons and with what justification did some people oppose peace with Spain?

6   What evidence is there in the extracts to suggest that James I was in a position of diplomatic strength in Europe in 1603?

The Treaty of London, negotiated by Robert Cecil at Somerset House, ended hostilities between England and Spain. The Venetian ambassador indicated some of the terms and problems.

6.3 Nicolo Molin, Venetian ambassador in England, to the doge and Senate, 14 July 1604

The main points of the terms of peace have, I am told, been settled thus:

The 30% on English goods to be removed, provided the goods are certificated as made in England; and a certificate shall also be required that all goods imported from Spain are sold in England, not elsewhere.

Flushing and Brill to remain in the hands of the English.   5

Free trade between England and all Spanish and Archducal possessions ...

Free trade between English and Dutch.

Two points are still open; one is the question of the Inquisition in search of forbidden books, which the Spanish claim to make; the other is, as to the amount of the assistance England may furnish to Holland. The Spanish insist on this point.   10
The King says that he would allow the Spanish to recruit in his kingdoms, but they would experience great difficulty in raising men; so intense is the hatred of the English for that nation.

Cal State Papers Venetian, vol. 10, p. 167

Questions

1   In what ways does **6.3** add to your knowledge of the motives for peacemaking in 1604?
2   What limitations were imposed on free trade between England and the Spanish possessions?
3   How was the issue of support for the Dutch resolved?
4   Why would the Spanish 'experience great difficulty in raising men' [**6.3, line 12**] if they recruited in James's kingdoms? Where might they find some support and for what reasons?
5   How far was the Treaty of London a diplomatic triumph for Cecil and James?

Anglo-Dutch relations

The Truce of Antwerp involved James in much diplomacy to end hostilities between Spain and Holland. It showed him as a mediator of European stature, a role confirmed in his attempts to avert war over the two Cleves–Jülich crises. A series of tetchy encounters between England and Holland ensued as the Dutch, no longer restrained by hostilities with Spain, could focus on extending trade and fishing to the detriment of England's interests.

The ambivalent nature of Anglo–Dutch relations is seen clearly in the years between 1609 and 1624: religion and history gave the two nations much in common; economic interests drove them apart. The Dutch emerged as the rivals of most English trading companies: Cockayne's New Company floundered partly because the Dutch refused to import English finished cloth; the Eastland Company was undermined by the Dutch in the Baltic; Levantine trade fell as Dutch ships brought spices via the Cape, and the Muscovy Company felt Dutch pressure.

Joel Benson (see recommended reading) describes Anglo–Dutch relations as moving from cooperation to competition at this time. The ambivalence and flexibility of James's policy is best seen in two issues: the fishing disputes in the middle years of the reign, and the Massacre of Amboyna of 1623.

Both nations had vested interests in fishing. A proclamation revoked Dutch privileges to fish herring off the English coast, enjoyed since the reign of Edward I, by demanding that alien fishermen pay for a licence to fish in English or Scottish waters. The Dutch retaliated with the arguments of Hugo Grotius's *Mare Liberum*, recently published to assert the freedom of the seas against Spain and Portugal, but equally appropriate against James I.

6.4 James's proclamation on fishing, Westminster, 6 May 1609

Whereas we have been contented since our coming to the Crown to tolerate a ...
liberty to all our friends whatsoever, to fish within our streams, and upon any of our
coasts of Great Britain, Ireland, and other adjacent islands, so far as the permission
or use thereof might not redound to the impeachment of our Prerogative Royal, not
to the hurt and damage of our loving Subjects ... So finding that our connivance ...   5
hath not only given occasion of over great encroachments upon our Regalities, or
rather questioning of our Right, but hath been a means of much daily wrongs to our
own people that exercise the trade of Fishing, as ... our Subjects are constrained to
abandon their fishing, or at the least are become so discouraged in the same, as they
hold it better for them to betake themselves to some other course of living, whereby   10
not only divers of our Coast towns are much decayed, but the number of mariners
daily diminished, which is a matter of great consequence to our Estate, considering
how how much the strength thereof consisteth in the power of Shipping and the use
of Navigation ... We have resolved that no person of any Nation or quality soever,

being not our natural born Subject, be permitted to fish upon any of the Coasts and   15
Seas of Great Britain, Ireland, and the rest of the Isles adjacent ... until they have ...
obtained Licences from us ...

Stuart Royal Proclamations. Royal Proclamations of King James I 1603–1625,
ed. J. F. Larkin and P. L. Hughes, 1973, vol. 1, no. 98, p. 217

Questions

1   How useful to the historian is a royal proclamation?
2   On what grounds expressed in the proclamation did James justify his
     actions? What did he mean by the term the prerogative royal?
3   What pressures, not specified in the proclamation, affected his decision
     to issue it?
4   How seriously did this proclamation threaten Dutch interests?

The economic rivalries were shelved when Protestantism in Europe was
threatened by the Cleves–Jülich crises and the assassination of Henry IV of
France, but Anglo-Dutch hostilities had emerged again, by the end of 1614, in
the stabler European situation when Dutch reaction to the Cockayne Project
provoked an aggressive attitude towards fishing licences.

Similar ambivalence in Anglo-Dutch relations can be seen in the matter of
Amboyna, an island in the East Indies where the English had sought to expand
trade. The governor of the Dutch East Indies, Jan Coen, regarded English
merchants in that area as interlopers. Some English merchants were executed
on Amboyna in February 1623 and, when news of the execution finally
reached England a year later, there were vigorous demands for retribution.
Again, however, the European situation determined policy: by 1624 a peaceful
solution to the Palatinate crisis was impossible and a Dutch alliance rather
than hostility was sought.

The Palatinate and the Spanish marriage

James persistently opted for diplomatic solutions to international crises;
dynastic marriages were a method of promoting harmony. While his elder son,
Prince Henry, was reluctant to marry the Spanish Infanta Anne, negotiations
for a Palatine marriage for the Princess Elizabeth indicated his goodwill to
German Protestants. The marriage took place at a crucial time, shortly after
the deaths of Prince Henry and Robert Cecil, and the arrival of Sarmiento
(Gondomar) as Spanish ambassador. His special relationship with the king

began a new era of Catholic conspiracy theories: Spain seeking to dominate England by the alienation of king from Parliament, and the pursuit of Spanish hegemony through a marriage of Prince Charles to the Infanta Maria. In reality, his relationship with Gondomar gave James the opportunity to keep his options open until 1624 in the great European crisis that began in 1618.

The outcome of the Palatinate marriage tested James's policies to the full, and ultimately found them wanting. He had viewed his son-in-law's acceptance of the throne of Bohemia with misgivings; he had procrastinated as his daughter and son-in-law were driven out of Prague by Habsburg forces after the Battle of the White Mountain. Maximilian of Bavaria's invasion of the Upper Palatinate on behalf of the Emperor, and the Spanish occupation of the Lower Palatinate, called for action as the dynastic interests of the Stuarts were threatened.

Lack of funds [5.29–5.31] made effective intervention impossible, although volunteers were raised. The report of the Council of War on the projected cost of intervention in 1621, and the parliamentary attitude towards subsidies, locked James into a diplomatic rather than a military course of action: the Spanish marriage project. The policy was not only deeply unpopular but produced real conflict between Crown and Parliament in 1621 when fundamental issues were raised on the nature of parliamentary privileges and royal prerogative over foreign policy.

6.5 Girolamo Lando, Venetian ambassador in England, to the doge and Senate, 30 April 1621

His Majesty now perceives that the whole weight of the recovery of the Palatinate will rest upon his shoulders alone; that he has as yet no preparations nor money or anything else necessary for taking an adequate army so far into the continent among the most vigorous forces of the Austrians; that he could receive no help; he has always had such an aversion for this ... that if he was cold before he now seems ice, 5
and if ever he inclined to negotiations he now thinks of nothing else ...

Cal State Papers Venetian, vol. 17, p. 36

6.6 Girolamo Lando, Venetian ambassador in England, to the doge and Senate, 7 May 1621

The Ambassador Gondomar expresses his intention of leaving here soon. Here he begins to say that it will be better for the negotiations about marriage and restitution [of the Palatinate] for him to be with his master at the time of Lord Digby's arrival to assist both ... [It] may suit the Spaniards better either that their ambassador should not be here or a new one who can offer excuses and gain time. However, as the 5
minister always acts with the most subtle artifice I do not know what to say, seeing

that he is so triumphant in all his negotiations, and although his art of bewitching owes more to the king's nature than his own skill, it would seem that he might count upon a continuance of irresolution, yet he does not seem to have great confidence in others.

Cal State Papers Venetian, vol. 17, p. 41

Questions

1   Why was James 'inclined to negotiations' in 1621 [**6.5, line 6**]?
2   What evidence is there in the letters of the Venetian ambassador to suggest that both England and Spain were playing for time during the crisis of 1621?
3   How does the Venetian ambassador in **6.6** convey his distrust of Gondomar? How significant was the influence of Gondomar on James's foreign policy?
4   Why were the Commons in 1621 keen that any action taken by James should not be directed solely at the Palatinate? How might this be said to imply a demand for a traditional Elizabethan policy against Spain?
5   How does James in **4.24** refute Phelips' justification for offering advice on foreign policy in **4.20**?
6   Was James's policy of raising troops for the Palatinate compatible with the idea of a Spanish marriage for Prince Charles?
7   How far would you agree that the Palatinate crisis provoked issues of fundamental importance in Crown–Parliament relations during the 1621 session?

Debates on the Palatinate produced a Parliament that sharpened fissures at home, politicising Puritanism and developing the parliamentary weapons of supply and impeachment. Rather than risk an ill-financed entry into war, James continued to support the increasingly elusive Spanish marriage scheme. He dissolved the Third Parliament to the delight of Gondomar whose strategy for preventing English intervention against Spain was clearly succeeding: England remained neutral while Spain preserved the 'family compact' with Austria (who might thereby be induced to help Spain against the Dutch on the expiry of the Truce of Antwerp) and kept a vital presence in the Palatinate to safeguard the 'Spanish Corridor'.

    The policy was of limited duration: events in Europe left the initiative firmly with the Habsburg bloc, making a successful outcome of the marriage negotiations impossible. Perhaps James realised this when he consented to the incognito mission of Charles and Buckingham to Madrid in 1623; the hasty enterprise seems out of character. Perhaps he was now old and ill and prepared to let Buckingham take the initiative. One way or another the mission would end the deadlock in marriage negotiations.

Ultimately the risks to the heir and the demands of the Spanish terms for the marriage proved too great. James's anxiety is shown in a letter to Charles and Buckingham [6.7].

6.7 James I to Charles, Prince of Wales, and the Marquis of Buckingham, Greenwich, 14 June 1623

My Sweet Boys

Your letter, by Cottington, hath stricken me dead. I fear it shall very much shorten my days, and I am the more perplexed that I know not how to satisfy my people's expectation here, neither know I what to say to the Council; for the fleet that staid upon a wind this fortnight ... must now be stayed, and I know not what reason I shall   5
pretend for the doing of it. But as for my advice and directions that you crave, in case they [the Spaniards] will not alter their decree [to delay the infanta's voyage to England], it is, in a word, to come speedily away, and if you can get leave, give over all treaty.

And this I speak without respect of any security they can offer you, except you never   10
look to see your old dad again, whom I fear you shall never see, if you see him not before winter. Alas, I now repent me sore that I ever suffered you to go away! I care for match,[1] nor nothing, so I may once have you in my arms again. God grant it, God grant it, God grant it! amen! amen! amen!

[1] match = the marriage between Prince Charles and the infanta

Intimate Letters of England's Kings, ed. Margaret Sanders, 1959, p. 64

6.8 Explanations given by the Duke of Buckingham for the king's reply to the declaration presented to him by both Houses of Parliament on 15 March 1624

My lord of Buckingham said that he taking the opportunity sometimes to speak from us to the King and sometimes again from the King to us where he saw he might do any good office, the king asked him why the parliament was so earnest to engage him in this business [breaking off the marriage negotiations and treaties with Spain] to which he answered that he conceived these to be the causes: first, the apprehension   5
of ambition of that great monarch of Spain ... And that in Germany they ... were jealous of the King of Spain's greatness, and especially of his footing in the Palatinate
...

Secondly he said the parliament was earnest in it because the conditions of the match were both prejudicial to the government at home, and also to our consciences.

R. Ashton, *James I by His Contemporaries*, 1969, p. 225

6.9 The secret clauses of the Spanish marriage treaty, July 1624

1 That particular Laws made against Roman Catholics, under which other Vassals of our realms are not comprehended … as likewise general Laws under which all are equally comprised, if so be they are such which are repugnant to the Romish religion, shall not at any time hereafter … be put into execution against the said Roman Catholics …   5

2 That no other Laws shall hereafter be made anew against the said Roman Catholics, but that there shall be a perpetual Toleration of the Roman Catholic Religion within private houses throughout all our Realms and Dominions, which we will have to be understood as well of our Kingdoms of Scotland and Ireland as in England …   10

3 That neither by us, nor by any other interposed person whatsoever, directly or indirectly, privately or publicly, will we treat (or attempt) anything with the most renowned Lady Infanta Donna Maria, which shall be repugnant to the Roman Catholic religion; Neither will we by any means persuade her that she should ever renounce or relinquish the same in substance or form …   15

4 That We and the Prince of Wales will interpose our authority, and will do as much as in us shall lie, that the Parliament shall approve, confirm, and ratify all the singular Articles in favour of the Roman Catholics, capitulated between the most renowned Kings by reason of this marriage; And that the said Parliament shall revoke and abrogate particular Laws made against the said Roman Catholics …

S. J. Houston, *James I*, 2nd edn, 1995, p. 129

Questions

1 What light do extracts **6.7** and **6.8** throw on the importance of Buckingham in foreign policy during the years 1623–24?

2 Using the extracts and your own knowledge, how would you argue that James I retained and exercised the power of policy-making in foreign affairs throughout his reign?

3 How does Buckingham's reply in **6.8** indicate that James's policy was set in a broad European dimension?

4 What was meant by the phrase 'the conditions of the match' [**6.8, line 8**]? Why might these conditions be seen as 'both prejudicial to the government at home, and also to our consciences' [**line 9**]?

5 In what ways would the secret marriage clauses be unacceptable to Parliament? In view of the failure of the trip to Madrid to secure the infanta's hand and arrival in England, and the growing pressure for breaking off treaties with Spain, why did James agree to such clauses?

The failure of the Spanish marriage made Charles and Buckingham heroes, if only for a short time, and leashed a spate of anti-Spanish propaganda on streets and stages throughout the capital.

6.10 Contemporary ballads

6.10(a)

I would to God his majesty
Of Spain were here awhile to see
The jollity of our English nation,
Then surely he would never hope
That either he or else the Pope   5
Could make here a Roman plantation.

6.10(b)

The Catholic King hath a little young thing
Called Donna Maria his sister,
Our Prince went to Spain her love to obtain,
But yet by good luck he hath missed her.

F. C. J. Hearnshaw, *English History in Contemporary Poetry*, 1926, p. 16

6.11 England and Spain as players on a chess board[1]

A game of chess is here displayed
Between the Black and White House made,
Wherein crown-thirsting policy
For the Black House, by fallacy,
To the White Knight check often gives,   5
And to some straits him thereby drives;
The Fat Bishop helps also,
With faithless heart, to give the blow:
Yet, maugre[2] all their craft, at length,
The White Knight, with wit-wondrous strength   10
And circumspective prudency,
Gives checkmate by discovery
To the Black Knight: and so at last,
The game thus won, the Black House cast
Into the bag, and therein shut,   15
Find all their plumes and cock-combs cut.
Plain dealing thus, by wisdom's guide,
Defeats the cheats of craft and pride.

[The play begins on the white part of the board (England), where it shows Jesuit designs against the Church of England (the White Queen's pawn); it ends in the black part of the board (Spain), where it shows the Spanish scheme to capture and convert Charles. In the following passage, the Black Knight describes Spain's insatiable appetite.]

And in the large feast of our vast ambition
We count but the White Kingdom, whence you come from,   20
The garden for our cook to pick his salads;
The food's lean France, larded with Germany;
Before which comes the grave, chaste signiory
Of Venice, served in, capon-like, in white broth;
From our chief oven, Italy, the bake-meats;   25
Savoy the salt, Geneva the chipt manchet;[3]
Below the salt the Netherlands are plac'd,
A common dish at the lower end o'the table
For meaner pride to fall to; for our second course,
A spit of Portugals served in for plovers;   30
Indians and Moors for blackbirds; all this while
Holland stands ready melted to make sauce
On all occasions.

[1] Thomas Middleton's *Game at Chess* is a splendid example of Catholic conspiracy theory. England is white, Spain black. White overcomes not only black, but fat – a reference to the Archbishop of Spalato, a man who had converted to Protestantism, found refuge in England, and then reverted his allegiance to Rome.
[2] maugre = in spite of
[3] chipt manchet = a type of bread

T. Middleton,*The Game at Chess***, 1624, ed. T. H. Howard, 1995, Act V, Scene 3**

Questions

1   What do the ballads show to be the main fear of ordinary citizens at the prospect of a Spanish marriage in 1624?
2   How does Middleton use language, style and imagery to convey the idea of a Spanish conspiracy?
3   How might you argue that these ballads reflect a 'country' culture whereas Middleton is writing for a sophisticated 'court' culture?
4   What fears are common to the authors of **6.10** and **6.11**?

By the end of 1624, James's policy towards Spain lay shattered as Buckingham attempted to make an anti-Habsburg alliance of England, Holland and France. Once again rivalry with the Dutch, this time over Amboyna, was set aside in the interests of wider international considerations.

Diplomatic exchanges in the early 1620s indicate the complexity and inter-dependence of English, Dutch and Spanish relations in a hostile Europe.

6.12 Girolamo Lando, Venetian ambassador, describing England, 21 September 1622

His Majesty ... has fallen out with the Dutch over the injuries his subjects have received from them, and has tried his utmost to secure for his people a share not only in the pearls and spices but in the forts and ports, acquired and settled at great cost of life. And yet it brings them nothing but vexation and hard knocks and absorbs a large quantity of gold, which does not return, in exchange for spices, and causes   5
great waste among the sailors, eight dying out of every ten. They are defeated in the rivalry for that trade as they do not go with strong forces to match those of the Dutch, and the agreements arranged have never produced good results ...

Cal State Papers Venetian, vol. 17, p. 425

6.13 Alvise Valaresso, Venetian ambassador in England, to the doge and Senate, 10 February 1623

Once and for all the Dutch ambassadors have brought their negotiations about the Indies to a final completion. It is certainly of no small matter that the ship, so long tossed among the rocks of public interests and by the winds of private passions, should arrive safe in the port of settlement without shipwreck. The claims of the English were not entirely satisfied. Necessity compelled the Dutch to yield much.   5
His Majesty acted between them, but chiefly I fancy by his inveterate and almost inseparable desire for peace with everyone. The Dutch have to pay £80,000 within three months ... When the ambassadors took leave of his Majesty he said a great deal to them in a set speech in full Council about the affection he will always bear the states, with many thanks for their hospitality to his children, and many promises to   10
reinstate them in their dominions by means of negotiation, or failing that by arms, adding that if he did not he would be considered an unnatural monster. But these ideas are empty bodies making nothing but sound. To the warm instances of the ambassadors for some help against so powerful an enemy he answered that he was not omnipotent and it was a great advantage for them to take as many soldiers as they   15
desired from his dominions.

Cal State Papers Venetian, vol. 17, p. 563

6.14 Dudley Carleton to John Chamberlain, The Hague, 21 March 1622/23

But when I consider that Spain and these United Provinces are at this present the two most diametrically opposite and hostile countries of the whole world and that the two only children of the king our sovereign are, one with the one, the other with the other, it passeth my capacity how they can be long well looked on in both places.

From Dudley Carleton to John Chamberlain, 1603–24, Jacobean Letters, ed. M. Lee, 1972, p. 298

Questions

1   Using the information from the extracts and your own knowledge, how would Anglo-Dutch hostility benefit Spain during the years 1618–24?

2   What European developments precipitated the policy of James I identified by ambassador Lando in **6.12**?

3   Why were the Dutch keen to secure English goodwill by 1621? What measures had they adopted to achieve this by 1623?

4   How would you explain the slight shift in English foreign policy indicated in **6.13**?

5   Why was Carleton anxious in **6.14**? How had the situation arisen that the Princess Elizabeth was at the Hague and Prince Charles in Spain?

6   What pressures forced James to ignore demands for revenge against the Dutch for the massacre of Amboyna in favour of an alliance with them by 1624?

A French marriage treaty was negotiated to spite Spain; it came as Mansfeld's mercenaries were leaving to try to relieve the Palatinate. James never wanted the war that ensued after the 1624 Parliament. His speeches show the dogged common sense that had characterised much of his foreign policy since 1604 and the sound appreciation that England did not have the capacity for successful intervention in Europe.

6.15   The response of James to the demand from the 1624 Parliament to break off the Spanish match

He is an unhappy man, that shall advise a King to war; and it is an unhappy thing to seek that by blood, which may be had by peace. Besides, I think your intentions are not to engage me in war, but withal you will consider how many things are requisite thereunto ... [James then outlined the costs he faced from the Spanish journey, his debts, the cost of ambassadors, aid to the Palatinate, Ireland, the navy and his children] ... In the meantime, my customs are the best part of my revenue, and in effect the substance of all I have to live on; all of which are farmed out upon that condition, that if there be a war, those bargains are to be disannulled ... [He explained how subsidies would take a long time to collect and he would be forced to borrow] ... This being the case, to enter into a war without sufficient means to support it, were to shew my teeth, and do not more ...   10

I will deal frankly with you: shew me the means how I may do what you would have of me, and if I take a resolution by your advice to enter into a war, then yourselves by your own deputies shall have the disposing of the money; I will not meddle with it, but you shall appoint your own treasurers. I say this with a purpose to invite you to   15
open your Purses ... If upon your offer I shall find the means to make the war

honourable and safe, and that I promise you in the word of a King, that although war and peace be peculiar prerogatives of kings, yet, as I have advised with you in the Treaties on which war may ensue, so I will not treat nor accept of a Peace, without first acquainting you with it.

J. Rushworth, *Historical Collections*, 1659, vol. 1, pp. 128–31

Questions

1   How does James I in **6.15** illustrate the disadvantages of a war policy?
2   How far does **6.15** reveal a greater spirit of cooperation between Crown and Parliament than shown in **4.20**, **4.23** and **4.24**?
3   How important were the concessions that James offered in return for sufficient supplies for war?
4   In what ways does the importance that James attached to revenue from customs help you to understand his attitude to Spain and the Dutch before 1618?
5   **6.15** shows that James was very clearly aware of the cost of war with Spain; how might those in Parliament in favour of war present an economic incentive to involvement in such a war?
6   When war became imminent, James's policy of the last twenty years was ruined. To what extent do you consider the reversal of his policy of the Treaty of London to mark a revolution in English foreign policy?

Ultimately, any popular and parliamentary hopes of hitting Spain on the high seas could offer little hope to the Palatinates in exile at the Hague. James's son's dismal interventionist policies, and their repercussions at home, proved the wisdom of his own attempts to be at best Rex Pacificus, at worst the exponent of masterly inactivity.

Recommended reading

S. L. Adams, 'Foreign policy and the Parliaments of 1621 and 1624', *Faction and Parliament*, ed. K. Sharpe, 1978
J. Benson, *Cooperation to Competition: English Perspective and Policy on Anglo-Dutch Economic Relations during the Reign of James I*, 1990
M. Breslow, *The Mirror of England* , 1970
C. Carter, 'Gondomar: ambassador to James I', *Historical Journal*, vol. 7, 1964
C. Carter, *The Secret Diplomacy of the Habsburgs*, 1964
T. Cogswell, 'Thomas Middleton and the court, 1624: a game at chess in context', *Huntington Library Quarterly*, vol. 48, 1984
R. Cust and A. Hughes, *Conflict in Early Stuart England*, 1989

P. Lake, 'Constitutional consensus and Puritan opposition in the 1620s: Thomas Scott and the Spanish match', *Historical Journal*, vol. 25, 1982

R. Lockyer, *Buckingham: The Life and Political Career of George Villiers, First Duke of Buckingham, 1592–1628*, 1981

C. Russell, *Parliaments and English Politics, 1621–24*, 1979

C. Russell, 'Foreign policy debate in the House of Commons, 1621', *Historical Journal*, vol. 20, 1977

7 'Not a bad king after all?' James I and the historians

James VI has had a much better press than James I. Seen in the Scottish perspective he was infinitely more successful than his predecessor and escaped the odium of his son's religious policy in Scotland. In his southern kingdom the image that Elizabeth had cultivated in her court of herself as a glorious, divine muse was a hard act for a foreign king to follow. In a number of areas, James was compared unfavourably with Elizabeth.

As centrifugal forces within present-day Britain counter the centripetal forces of Britain's position within Europe, it is natural that the Union of the English and Scottish kingdoms should be probed. This British dimension is currently the most exciting development in historical research. While James I certainly drew upon skills acquired as James VI, during his lifetime the kingdoms were united in little other than his person [7.3–7.5]. The researches of J. Wormald, C. Russell and G. Donaldson indicate that the good will on the part of James for union was rarely reciprocated by his contemporaries and that, for them, the concept of *British* history was elusive. Even that genius of the Scottish Enlightenment, David Hume, made the southern kingdom the focus of a history of Britain. James took the title King of Great Britain in the hope that this would create unity by an appeal to the heroic past. Anglo-Scottish hostility was deep-rooted, but the real xenophobes on both sides were worried members of the elite, afraid of losing perks [7.6]. Interesting avenues for exploration lie in the concepts of 'English' and 'Scottish' national feeling in 1603, especially in the border areas.

Traditional views of James and his dealings with Parliament from the early Whig writings of Macaulay through to W. Notestein and D. H. Willson [7.7, 7.8] have been challenged by C. Russell [7.9], whose writings have inspired many much needed and scholarly researches into the early Stuart Parliaments and court [7.6, 7.11]. Aspects of this so-called 'revisionism' have in turn been challenged by T. Rabb [7.10] and T. Cogswell [7.14].

James I has been largely exonerated as the inept ruler who placed the nation on the high road to Civil War through his bunglings with Parliament. In religious affairs, the idea put forward by D. H. Willson that a 'deep fissure' appeared in the Jacobean Church has been rejected by a long series of research articles culminating in the work of K. Fincham and P. Lake [7.17].

Rehabilitation in the area of foreign policy has shown James less of a coward toadying to Spain than a sincere king pursuing a pacific policy of *Realpolitik*, only too aware of the real cost of intervention.

There is always the possibility that James I has been over-revised. It is at least agreed, however, that a financial whitewash is not feasible. The last word should lie with M. Lee, whose conclusion is that while James I slobbered at the mouth and had favourites he was 'not such a bad king after all' [7.18].

7.1 A blend of qualities and defects

James VI indeed had many qualities ... Good-humoured and good natured, he was honestly desirous of increasing the prosperity of his subjects. His mental powers were of no common order; his memory was good, and his learning, especially on theological points, was by no means contemptible. He was intellectually tolerant, anxious to be at peace with those whose opinions differed from his own. He was   5 above all things eager to be a reconciler, to make peace where there had been war before, and to draw those to live in harmony who had hitherto glared at one another in mutual defiance. He was penetrated with a strong sense of the evil of fanaticism.

These merits were marred by grave defects. He was too self-confident to give himself the pains to unravel a difficult problem, and had too weak a perception of the   10 proportional value of things to enable him to grasp the important points of a case to the exclusion of those which were merely subsidiary. With a thorough dislike of dogmatism in others, he was himself the most dogmatic of all men, and – most fatal of all defects in a ruler – he was ready to conceive the worst of those who stood up against him ... Warmly affectionate ... he never attached himself to any man who was   15 truly great. He mistook flattery for devotion ... It was easy for his favourites to abuse his good-nature, provided that they took care not to wound his self-complacency.

S. R. Gardiner, *The History of England from the Accession of James I to the Outbreak of the Civil War, 1603–1642*, 1883, vol. 1, p. 48

7.2 Closer to greatness than many men

James Stuart was never a great man, yet in his absurdity he is more like a twisted shape of greatness than many more ordinary men. He had tolerance and laughter and knowledge and intelligence; he liked men and women, he desired great things. The gossips and controversialists laughed and sneered, and our generations follow them. Yet once at least, in the midst of so much pleasant mirth, it is permissible to   5 remember that Francis Bacon praised James Stuart living and John Donne lamented him dead, and that it is not safe too easily to despise a man they honoured, though he were the King, nor wise too easily to suppose that they honoured him with a servile insincerity, because he was the King.

Charles Williams, *James I*, 1934, p. 298

Questions

1 In what ways and to what extent were the merits of James VI as outlined
   by S. R. Gardiner [7.1] likely to be beneficial to Britain in 1603?
2 While Gardiner refers to 'many qualities' [line 1], he qualifies the king's
   defects as 'grave' [line 9]. In the light of the information in the above
   extracts and your own knowledge, how far would you say that the merits
   of James I as king were outweighed by his defects?

7.3 The absentee king

James VI's departure for London in April 1603 amidst scenes of great emotion
looked like the high point of Scottish pride. The Scots had given their 'auld enemies'
a king, and thus provided the final answer to the aggression of Edward I, Edward III,
and Henry VIII. James, through the medium of his coinage, allowed himself a
pardonable boast, with the smug little motto 'Henricus rosas regna Jacobus' (Henry   5
[VII united] the roses, James the kingdoms). It was all very gratifying. It also created
an immense problem: absentee kingship. It is a remarkable tribute to James's ability
as King of Scotland that he succeeded as well as he did ... The fact that he returned
only once, in 1617, has given rise to the myth that in his enthusiasm for the English
crown he forgot all about his northern kingdom. It was quite the reverse. He went to   10
England determined to maintain the interests of that kingdom ... He had a dream of
a united nation, in which Scottish merchants, Scottish lawyers, Scottish councillors
would play a full part. He failed; the English merchants were determined to keep out
the beggarly and importunate Scots, and the English and Scottish lawyers were, on
the whole, sufficiently satisfied with their own tradition. He did not even succeed in   15
retaining close personal ties; after the first decade, when he surrounded himself with
Scots, the resentment of the English courtiers forced him to send them home. Yet he
kept his channels of communication open, writing endless letters to his council and
demanding information from it; these flowed between Edinburgh and London with
new speed, because of the efficient postal service that he set up ... And at the end of   20
his life, in ill health and worn down by the frustrations of his English rule, he turned
back to his original kingdom. In 1621, when his English Parliament was obsessed
with the burning issue of foreign policy, and frustrated by James's refusal to give a
clear lead as the defender of the Reformed Church, the king was heavily involved in
pushing his ecclesiastical policy, the Five Articles of Perth, through a reluctant, even   25
hostile Scottish Parliament.

J. Wormald, *Court, Kirk, and Community: Scotland 1470–1625*, 1981, p. 191

7.4 Problems left by Elizabeth

As James's difficulties in England multiplied in his later years, he may sometimes
have been in doubt as to which of his kingdoms was 'easiest to be ruled'; all his
experience certainly justified his forecast in 1603 that 'the augmentation' would be
'but in cares and heavy burdens'. But the cares and burdens were not of James's

making; they constituted the *damnosa hereditas*[1] left by Elizabeth Tudor, a sovereign   5
utterly careless of the well being of her kingdom after her own demise, who had
allowed unsolved problems to pile up in her later years and whose reign had ended
in anti-climax, in decline, almost in failure. James went to a country heading for
insolvency, and one in which the whole system of government was already being
challenged. For example, Elizabeth had belatedly seen the danger of Puritanism, but   10
it was left to James to redefine Anglicanism and indeed to reconstruct the Church
of England on a non-Puritan foundation which was to endure. James's reign also
brought peace with Spain, the pacification of Ireland and the first permanent English
colony in America. His logic and commonsense were not appreciated by his more
emotional English subjects, but the fact is that problems which Gloriana never solved   15
were solved by this king from Scotland.

[1] *damnosa hereditas* = Elizabeth I's cursed legacy to James I

G. Donaldson, *Scotland James V–James VII*, 1990, p. 236

7.5 Relative failure to unite England and Scotland

[The] accession of James VI of Scotland as James I of England, by virtue of his
descent ... from Henry VII, did not in any organic sense unite the two crowns far
less the two realms. Until his death in 1625 James Stewart remained James VI, King
of Scots, even though on 25 July 1603 he was anointed and crowned in Westminster
Abbey as 'James the First, King of England, Scotland, France and Ireland'. Indeed,   5
strenuous efforts by James to unite the realms of England and Scotland failed, and
their general laws and administration remained separate and distinct, as did their
crowns and the rules of succession thereto.

All this retains its validity in spite of the fact that James assumed the style of King of
Great Britain, which became accepted diplomatic usage. The term 'Great Britain' to   10
distinguish the island of Britain from the Little Britain of the continent, Brittany,
had long been current and was sufficiently widely known to be used by Cervantes in
1604. But, as was wittily said at that time, James's self-bestowed title (which was a
second thought, for he had toyed with the notion of calling himself emperor) made
the British Solomon a king without a kingdom, thus possibly attracting the attention   15
of the author of Don Quixote.

William Ferguson, *Scotland's Relations with England: A Survey to 1707*, 1977,
p. 97

Questions

1   'A king without a kingdom' [7.5, line 15]. Was the title 'King of Great
Britain' anything more than an empty one? How appropriate is the image
of James VI and I as a Don Quixote forever striving to dominate events
over which he had no control?

2   How far would you support the argument that James's union of the kingdoms was the best that could be expected in the circumstances?

3   How would you support Donaldson's argument that the 'cares and … burdens' [7.4, line 4] that James anticipated in 1603 were not of his own making?

4   What were the advantages and disadvantages for Scotland of an absentee king?

Parliament

7.6 Parliamentary opposition

The domestic scene, unlike the foreign, was dominated by two great issues – the union and finance – and the settlement of these questions was in turn conditioned by the constant presence, actual or potential, of a Parliament unprecedented in lengths of sittings, overall duration and frequency of calling since that of 1529–36.

Two things are clear in this. First, whatever the 'revisionists' may argue, there was   5
opposition. The opposition, moreover, was structured and principled; it almost always commanded a majority in the Commons and latterly in the Lords as well, and it was focused explicitly on the two key issues of government policy: Union, which lay closest to the king's heart, and fiscal reform, which was … Cecil's principal concern. Second … the Bedchamber settlement played a crucial role in triggering   10
and sustaining this opposition. The settlement itself, which consigned the bedchamber wholly to the Scots, was … James's initial riposte to the failure of the English political establishment to embrace union wholeheartedly; and thereafter the king's exclusively Scottish inner entourage became a prime sticking point in relations with Parliament, especially where supply was concerned.

David Starkey (ed.), *The English Court from the Wars of the Roses to the Civil War*, **1987, p. 262**

7.7 Poor parliamentary management

During the years between 1603 and 1621 many things served indirectly to force a new leadership. James did much to put his Government on the defensive, much that tended to create an offensive upon the part of those who had complaints to make.

Everyone knows that James had trouble to make ends meet. It was not only that he was rather free in distributing gifts to friends and favourites. Government had grown   5
more expensive, as it is always doing. In the natural course of events, he was forced to ask for more money than had ever been requested by his thrifty predecessor. He failed to get it, and through the bestowal of patents and monopolies upon favourites, and the laying of impositions, raised some money and raised as well the price of living. The knights and burgesses who came up to Westminster brought with them   10
from their constituents stories of the abuses of patentees and royal officials …

All this is well known. But it explains why the House of Commons became vociferous about grievances … The Commons urged their grievances and Privy Councillors, who sought to minimise the extent of those grievances, or to explain how the King had been in ignorance of them, found themselves naturally thrown on 15 the defensive, while those who enlarged upon grievances were gaining the lead of the House …

No one thing did more to put the Commons on the offensive and Privy Councillors on the defensive than the Committee of the Whole for Grievances …

James's personal relations with the Parliament did not a little to put the Commons on 20 the offensive. His want of dignity in carriage was no greater handicap to him than his want of dignity in political conduct. Elizabeth had held herself in the background, appearing at the beginning and at the end of sessions, occasionally sending a message … It was not so with James. His itch for meddling and for utterance made it impossible for him to remain in the background … Royal words lost their weight. 25 High-flown language about kingship and prerogative brought quiet smiles at first … but, when often repeated, stirred resentment and provoked rebuttal … Few kings have been so fitted by nature to call forth an opposition and to put Government on the defensive. It was a further blunder of James that he neglected to retain in the Lower House enough Councillors … of ability and tact … 30

Hardly less important a factor in the decline of the influence of the Council in the Commons was the failure of that body to look after elections …

Wallace Notestein, 'The winning of the initiative by the House of Commons', *Proceedings of the British Academy*, **1926, pp. 31ff.**

7.8 Growing demand for fundamental change

The fissure between King and Commons may be seen in the divergent approach to grievances. James's Government brought abuses which the Commons were not slow to point out, and the redress of grievances became their constant theme. But grievances meant more than new abuses. Things that had been suffered under Elizabeth now appeared outmoded and intolerable, and the time seemed ripe for their 5 reform. Often they involved a diminution of royal authority or revenue, and thus grievances merged with a demand for fundamental change, change that would shift power from Crown to Parliament …

How abysmal was his ignorance of the English House of Commons! It was, he discovered, a formidable body that challenged his prerogative; but he never fathomed 10 the sources of its strength, the growing effectiveness of its procedure and leadership, or the inevitability of its advance to power.

D. H. Willson, *King James VI and I*, **1956, pp. 246ff.**

Questions

1 'Few kings have been so fitted by nature to call forth an opposition' [7.7, lines 27–28]. How far does the personality of James explain the problems identified by Notestein in Crown–Parliament relations?

2 'The fissure between King and Commons may be seen in the divergent approach to grievances' [7.8, lines 1–2]. How far do you agree with this view of D. H. Willson?

7.9 James's Parliament – not a high road to Civil War

The conventional belief that the Parliaments of 1604–29 were a 'high road to Civil War' logically implies two further beliefs. One is the belief that Parliament was a powerful institution; it is only if Parliament is thought of as a great power in the State that it can be made to fill the role for which it is cast, as a potential challenger to the king for supreme power. The other logical necessity to the belief that this period was a 'high road to Civil War' is the belief that the Parliaments of these years witnessed a constitutional struggle between two 'sides', Government and opposition, or, in modern language, court and country. Two sides are an essential condition of a Civil War, and where there are not two sides, there cannot be a high road to Civil War.   10

These two beliefs are logically implied in statements made by well-known historians, and these implications have gained the status of received opinions. 'Every schoolboy knows', that Parliament was growing more powerful in the early Stuart period, and that it was divided into supporters of 'government' and 'opposition'. It is the contention of this article that these two beliefs are false. Before 1640, Parliament was   15 not powerful, and it did not contain an 'opposition'.

Conrad Russell, 'Parliamentary history in perspective, 1604–1629', *History*, **vol. 61, 1976, p. 3**

7.10 Effective opposition – not faction

Cannot the term 'opposition' be descriptive without necessarily implying a resounding Whig view of English history? In James I's reign, for example, there were concerns about such policies of the court as impositions and the Spanish match, anxieties which went beyond factional manoeuvres and local interests and united a substantial body of MPs. Is there a better word to describe their views than   5 'opposition'? The implication that, because there was no real 'opposition' there was little conflict, or expectation of conflict, pin-points the real danger of this approach, and again justifies a preference for the old view, warts and all, over the full-blown version of the new …

Those who opposed their rulers held 'opposition' beliefs and supported one another   10 in 'opposition' groups, whether organised and systematic or not. Nor did contemporaries fail to see what was happening: the Earl of Northampton, for

instance, spoke of an MP who in 1604–10 'opposed the king so powerfully in the Parliament'. Of course the concerns and the alliances changed, depending on the issue at hand. But the ability of these 'opponents' to persuade fellow MPs to act   15
effectively in concert is beyond question. One has but to follow the manoeuvrings that, for example, produced the Apology in 1604, the attack on the undertakers in 1614, the Protestation of 1621, or the impeachment of Cranfield in 1624, to see that careful, coordinated tactics were at work. A favourite stratagem, for instance, was to use a recess, when there was time to lay plans, to prepare a beautifully orchestrated   20
assault on some grievance as soon as the House reassembled.

T. Rabb, 'Revisionism revised: two perspectives on early Stuart parliamentary history', *Past and Present*, no. 92, 1981, p. 66

7.11 James's favourites and faction

James I is famous as the King who indulged favourites who undermined the Tudor monarchy and polity. Until 1621 (at the earliest), however, James's favourites neither enjoyed free rein, nor wielded great political power, nor immunised the King from the conversation and counsel of other courtiers and factions. It was Villiers who broke the mould. His early career was conventional enough: the client of a magnate   5
faction and attractive to James more for his physical than intellectual qualities, Villiers appeared the archetypal courtier – the puppet of favour more than the puppeteer of patronage. But Villiers was ambitious for power. Having dabbled in alliances with the nobility, he turned, after 1621, to construct at court an independent following of men who were his creatures rather than his clients.   10
Moreover he strove to block the advancement of all who were outside his circle of patronage and, after 1623, all who disagreed with his policy.

Kevin Sharpe, 'Faction at the early Stuart court', *History Today*, vol. 33, p. 43

7.12 The role of Buckingham

In early Stuart England the most obvious example of a favourite was George Villiers, Duke of Buckingham. He first appeared on the scene in 1614 at a time when Robert Carr, Earl of Somerset, was in the ascendant, but by 1616 he had toppled Carr and established himself as supreme in the King's affections. Contemporary observers, whose opinion has coloured the later judgement of historians, assumed that over the   5
course of the next two or three years Buckingham became in effect a Valido, the *de facto* source of authority in the English State. Such a development would only have been possible, however, if James had given up the reins of Government, but there was never any question of this. James had been a king virtually since the day he was born, and he took it for granted that God had not only appointed him to rule but had   10
also given him the capacity to do so. It was a trust he could not and would not relinquish.

R. Lockyer, 'An English Valido? Buckingham and James I', *For Veronica Wedgwood These: Studies in Seventeenth Century History*, ed. R. Ollard and P. Tudor-Craig, 1986, p. 49

7.13 James – a puppet of Gondomar?

But one thing we can be certain of: James's conduct with Gondomar was clearly not that of a puppet on a string. The contemporary critics of both claimed that James was putty in the hands of the ambassador, the Spanish Machiavelli, and historians since have repeated the tale. But Gondomar himself knew better. Toward the end of his embassy some French envoys in London, having failed to bring James into a war   5 contemplated against Spain in the Alps, claimed that they had found the king to be 'completely Spanish' and referred to him publicly as 'Don Jacques', a name the English Puritans quickly picked up (for cautious jocular use among themselves). Gondomar enjoyed the joke, but soberly told his sovereign that it would please him greatly if James more truly merited the 'Don'.

C. H. Carter, 'Gondomar: ambassador to James I', *Historical Journal,* **vol. 2, 1964, p. 208**

7.14 How powerful was Parliament in 1624?

Whether or not some variety of 'court' and 'country', however defined, describes action on the floor of the House, a much more fundamental question remains: was Parliament actually 'powerless' and not 'a great power in the State'? Russell has argued as much, and he is surely right to stress that Parliament was not in continuous existence before the Civil War … Parliament alone proved able to break   5 the Spanish hold on England, and it alone could lend credibility to the projects of a comparatively impotent monarch. In short the evidence from 1624 begs an obvious question; if Parliament was not a great power in the State in 1624, who or what was? While both king and Council had vast powers, both real or potential, neither was capable of resolving the diplomatic log-jam left in the wake of the abortive Anglo-   10 Spanish dynastic alliance. Certainly neither could produce sums of money running into six figures. In these circumstances, one would like to know the definition of 'great'. Russell's test of greatness is the ability of Parliament to tie redress of grievances to supply. In 1624, as we have seen, Parliament had little trouble passing Russell's test with flying colors. It was painfully clear that the only legislation the   15 Crown really wanted was the subsidy bill, and from this one overriding desire flowed a flood of concessions.

Thomas Cogswell, *The Blessed Revolution: English Politics and the Coming of War, 1621–1624,* **1989, p. 321**

Questions

1   Why do historians differ as to the nature of opposition in Jacobean Parliaments?

2   How useful is the term faction when considering pressures within Parliament and court during the reign of James I?

3   How important was Buckingham in generating faction in court and Parliament from 1614 until the death of James I? Was he a Valido?

4   How would you explain the influence of Gondomar at the English court? How significant was that influence?

5   To what extent do you support the view that preparations for war gave the 1624 Parliament a major initiative?

The Church

7.15 The Hampton Court Conference

But in truth the King had done great harm. He was a controversialist, thirsting for wordy victory, not the statesman who might find Puritan notions unacceptable but who would seek to avoid dissension and bitterness. He had first encouraged the Puritans, then called them to argue a case already decided against them and treated them with scorn and contumely. Conformity was to be more rigidly enforced; and   5
the Church was headed not towards greater comprehension but towards a hard and narrow exclusiveness. In this fateful decision the King's will was a vital factor.

Willson, *King James VI and I*, p. 208

7.16 The Puritans

The discontent of the Puritans found only too much to feed upon as the reign wore on. A deep fissure was appearing in the Church; and while the bishops turned to the King, the Puritans turned to Parliament.

Willson, *King James VI and I*, p. 210

7.17 James's management of ecclesiastical affairs

In his management of ecclesiastical affairs, James I combined a detailed grasp of abstract theory with a native political shrewdness. This is in stark contrast to his predecessor, who, for all her gifts of prevarication and deception, showed no interest in doctrinal theory or its relationship with the formulation of policy … James, however, was always ready to explain the assumptions on which his actions were   5
based, and such public expressions were a central plank of his whole strategy. The king emerges as a subtle manipulator of men and as a masterly short-term political operator, able to keep his options open almost indefinitely and any number of people guessing as to his real intentions. Indeed, it is difficult not to be impressed by the skill with which he handled both anti-Puritan and anti-papal stereotypes to create   10
the ideological space within which the royal will could manoeuvre and policy be formulated. Yet in many ways his strengths were also his weaknesses. Personal contact and management were central to his style of kingship, but James could overestimate the impact of his personality and arguments. He clearly overrated his dialectical and political talents and won arguments because he was king rather than   15
because he convinced his audience … James's desire to intervene dramatically to restore European peace came into conflict with the basic thrust of his ecclesiastical

policy, the defusing of 'radical' Puritanism and rabid anti-popery through the incorporation of the evangelical Calvinism into the Jacobean establishment. Faced with a clear choice, the king failed to realise that the one aim precluded the other.

K. Fincham and P. Lake, 'The ecclesiastical policy of King James I', *Journal of British Studies,* vol. 24, 1985, p. 206

Questions

1 How far does the author of **7.15** and **7.16** support the idea of a *damnosa hereditas* of Queen Elizabeth to James in religious matters?
2 To what extent did James I redefine the Anglican Church?
3 What criteria would you establish by which to measure James's achievements in religion? How far are your criteria met?
4 Consider the view that the religious policy of James VI and I was an advantage rather than a disadvantage to a king ruling multiple kingdoms.
5 To what extent do you consider that the religious policy of King James became untenable after the outbreak of the Thirty Years War?

7.18 A more stable kingdom – James's legacy

King James's favorites and courtiers, then, do not altogether deserve the bad press they have received in the traditional accounts. Their partial rehabilitation, if it can be called that, is one more aspect of the rehabilitation of the reputation of their master; it is encouraging that the historians of England are beginning to appreciate the merits of a ruler whose talents those who are primarily historians of Scotland have   5
long admired. Perhaps the very final word can be left to one of the latter, Dr Wormald, who is currently at work on a full-length study of James which will doubtless supersede Willson as the standard account. In England, she writes, 'he defused problems within the Church and the State, and thereby presided over a kingdom probably more stable than his predecessor had left, and certainly than his   10
successor was to rule'. The research surveyed herein suggests that historians' opinion is moving toward agreement with that verdict.

M. Lee Jr, 'James I and the Historians: not a bad king after all?', *Albion,* vol. 16, 1984

Question

1 In the light of your investigation into the character and statecraft of James I, King of Great Britain, how far do you accept the view expressed in **7.18**?

Index